TENDING the EPICUREAN GARDEN

TENDING the EPICUREAN GARDEN

Hiram Crespo

HUMANIST PRESS

WASHINGTON, DC

This book is dedicated

to all the Epicureans of the past, present and future

whose commitment to the teaching mission of the Gardens

has allowed our tradition to continue to flourish

Contents

I

WHERE IS WISDOM HIDING?
THE NEED FOR PHILOSOPHY TODAY

"¡Imprudente!" ... That is the word that my mother, and many proper Spanish ladies, used when I was growing up for people who lacked prudence and it's part of how we learned proper, common sense behavior. If a gossipy, nosy old woman didn't know when to shut her mouth, "¡Imprudente!" If the child of your house guests was running around and out of control, "¡Imprudente!" If a snotty pupil insulted his well-meaning teacher, "¡Imprudente!" ... and it was assumed that people had an intuitive understanding of what was expected and considered as prudent behavior.

I think part of why I love the word is that it's so much less insulting and obscene than most other words that could be used, perhaps even more accurately, to call out people in these situations. But also, those of us with a philosophical demeanor like to analyze life. I grew up cognizant that lack of prudence (*imprudencia*) was a bad thing, and that therefore everyone takes for granted that prudence is a value and a virtue, a good that should be sought for its own sake.

How in need of prudence many of us are! Throughout the years, I've encountered people who have no control, or desire to exert control, over their desires, who fall into habits of needless, excessive spending and amass mountains of debt that they couldn't possibly pay back.

If they do pay the debt back, it's through years of slavery at the end of which they have nothing to show for it. Maybe a home is good debt because it usually appreciates in value over the years and can be sold for a profit. But the latest electronic gadgets and computers, the most expensive cars, the overpriced clothes, these are goods that lose value the moment we begin to use them, and many gadgets have a built-in obso-lescence so that their makers expect us to consume updated versions of these goods in the future, after we've gotten habitu-ated to having them. Consumerism is at the root of much of the fiscal crisis that America is trying to recover from.

I've met people who have gotten involved in cults, and some who have survived a considerable amount of sexual and psychological abuse. Some feel that the benefits of being reli-gious outweigh the harm, or that they could not possibly live without their faith, that they would be disowned by their fam-ilies and communities. Many are genuinely good people try-ing to live good lives who believe in the essential harmlessness of their particular religion and do not wish to be burdened with examples of religious tyranny in its name.

I've also encountered throughout the years people who overeat, who develop bad habits of consumption that destroy their health and reputation, who speak too much and too early, and because I've had the pleasure of also knowing pru-dent people and of learning from my own mistakes and from others' mistakes, I've been able to contrast the lives and nar-ratives of different groups of people and discern the healthier ways of making choices. I've developed my own wisdom tradi-tion and art of living. Prudence is gained from almost every kind of experience.

People who are already familiar with Epicureanism will probably find it interesting that the neighborhood where I grew up is known as "Jardines," which translates as "Gardens." I did not grow up in an Epicurean Garden but I guess, in some way, Gardens will always sound like my home and remind me of my roots.

When I learned about Epicureanism, it seemed like all the common sense ideas that I had come to believe had coalesced like the auspicious constellations of prophecy aligning in 2012. But it doesn't take an aboriginal shaman to see how the medicine of Epicureanism can heal our world. All it takes is a little prudence.

Prudence comes from a Latin word which is a shorter form of *providentia*, the ability to see ahead, to have foresight and to prepare for the future. The Merriam-Webster dictionary defines it as "the ability to govern and discipline oneself by the use of reason". The Greek word for it used by early Epicureans was *phronesis*, and was generally translated simply as practical wisdom.

How to Use this Book Effectively

This is a book about practical wits: an invitation to delve into Epicurean practice and, ultimately, to develop your own wisdom tradition. In fact, it is an exuberant celebration of prudence and where she takes you. Although I go into the history and doctrine of our tradition, in this book I do not intend to present Epicureanism as a history of itself but as a handbook for the daily practice of our system of philosophy for people who may or may not have a community of philosopher friends. I am presenting Epicureanism as an ancient wisdom tradition that has been adapted for our age.

The Society of Friends of Epicurus was founded to reinstate the teaching mission of the Epicurean Gardens and to ensure the cultural continuity of our tradition. This requires an initial adaptation, expansion, and immersion process in order to allow a new, culturally vibrant and relevant wisdom tradition to organically strengthen its roots just like a new garden being nurtured in new soil.

If you develop as much passion for Epicureanism as I have, think about the care that newly planted trees require. Like all gardening, applied philosophy is a life-long process, a practice of frequent pruning and watering. So it is with our bad and good habits. As we become cognizant of the perturbances that impede our happiness and tranquility, we develop a resolve to slowly reinvent ourselves.

I encourage the keeping of a diary or journal as you read this book in order to facilitate the analyzed life, to ponder the meaning and usefulness of Epicurean teachings, and to develop and apply the ideas presented here. At the end of the book, if its content is properly assimilated and applied, the reader would have at least the beginnings of a wisdom tradition, a tool kit for dealing with life's baggage and difficulties, and a series of social and introspective tasks to complete, some of which require a life-long commitment. It is my intention to be a friendly presence helping the reader to establish herself on her own path as a philosopher, whether or not she ultimately chooses to call herself an Epicurean.

The book is intended as an interactive experience. At the end of each chapter, I will propose a set of tasks to apply the knowledge covered. Some of these tasks are introspective and best addressed through journaling and inner work, whereas others are social. You will benefit the most from this book if you complete these tasks and use them as starting points in your practice of philosophy.

On the Need for an Evolving Epicurean Tradition

Any pragmatic introduction to the modern application of the philosophical theory of Epicurus in daily life requires a recognition of the need for updating old ideas. I will honor the voice of Epicurus, Lucretius, Philodemus, Thomas Jefferson and other Epicureans of the past but will also present my own independent, contemporary assessment of our tradition. I will also attempt to update the teachings in light of contemporary scientific research on well-being and happiness, and wherever the ideas of the old school are stale or irrelevant I will propose alternative views that modern Epicureans can evaluate and adapt as independent philosophers.

In other words, as much as we look up to our Master as one would a guru, very few modern Epicureans see Epicureanism as mere deification of our culture hero and blind obedience to him. We're more likely to see our tradition as a living, changing set of conversations that began with Epicurus and will continue for all of history, as well as the frugal, simple, and pleasant lifestyles rich in wisdom and friendship that are inspired by this wholesome discourse.

It is obvious that the early atomism of Epicurus, for instance, is quite different from the modern one of physics. In the necessary and inevitable process of updating Epicurean teaching and tradition, I have subjected the potential innovations to the criteria given by Epicurus (Erler, 2011) dealing with innovation and forbidding the "muddling" of doctrines that disagree with each other. The two guidelines provided by Epicurus are *akoloythia* and *symphonia*, which translate as "consistency" (has no internal contradictions) and "coherence" (is in sympathy with the rest of Epicurus' doctrine).

I will, from the onset, admit the influence of Buddhist doctrine and of the contemplative practices and theories of the Zen school, much of which resonates deeply with our own tradition and could considerably enrich future Epicureanism. I have also drawn inspiration from the heterodox materialist school of philosophy within Hinduism, known as Carvaka.

Epicureanism is a philosophy of the people and for the people. Therefore, I intend to challenge common conceptions of what it means to be a philosopher and to argue that we are all potential philosophers. Our philosophy is therapeutic, utilitarian, and practical. It is for everyone who wishes to develop an art of living, regardless of social class, gender, sexual orientation, or other considerations.

In our society's education system, we generally do not learn about philosophy, happiness and ethics (the field of philosophy that is concerned with the good life) as part of school curriculum. We are illiterate when it comes to the good life and the most wholesome ways to procure it. In fact, there isn't even a word in our language for the science of happiness in the same way that biology is the science of life and psychology is the science of the mind.

Many of the words Epicurus used, such as hedonism, have come to mean something very different today as a result of centuries of defamation and obscurity. In order to rescue the cultural treasure of Epicureanism, we need to invent and reclaim terminology that has been misused or neglected such as suavity, faith, ataraxia, hedonism, aponia, etc. We must restore the original meaning of these words, and perhaps even coin new English verbiage so that a new paradigm can properly take root in our day and the Gardens can flourish again.

Ergo, I will refer to ethics broadly as our science of well-being, which leads to the good life, and I will also introduce, from time to time, new verbiage so that we can start naming and addressing things that we aren't used to addressing. At the end of each chapter, the new terminology that has been introduced will be highlighted again. As part of your process of developing a new set of habits that lead to a pleasant life, pay special attention to these new words and what they name. Begin to incorporate them into your lifestyle and mode of thinking.

New Verbiage:

Prudence

References:

Erler, Michael. "Autodidact and student: on the relationship of authority and autonomy" in Fish, Jeffrey and Sanders, Kirk, eds., *Epicurus and the Epicurean Tradition* (New York: Cambridge University Press, 2011).

II

EPICURUS OF SAMOS AND HIS LEGACY

Epicurus of Samos and the Ancient School

Honoring a sage is itself a great good to the one who honors.
– Vatican Sayings

Epicurus of Samos, our cheerful Hegemon (leader) whose name means "ally" or "friend," was born in the Greek island of Samos and lived between the years 341 and 270 BCE. His mother Chairestrate had been a folk healer, an experience which apparently taught him to distrust supernatural claims. His father Neocles had been a school teacher.

For four years, Epicurus studied under the Platonist Pamphilus of Samos. After his instructor was unable to clearly explain the concept of original chaos, which was an important feature of the Greek creation myth, he began to develop strong anti-Platonic views and began to articulate the need for a scientific, naturalist cosmology.

Epicurus began to study philosophy between the ages of 14-17 in the city of Teos under Nausiphanes, which places Epicurus under the lineage of Nausiphanes' instructor, the renowned atomist and materialist Democritus. The main reform that Epicurus would make to the early atomist teaching would be the theory of the swerve, which had the immediate effect of negating the predeterminism of early atomists. Otherwise, Epicurus' doctrine falls neatly within the tradition of the ancient atomists.

We also know that Epicurus shared his teacher's criticism of Pyrrho and the Skeptics, a school that proposed that knowledge was not attainable or desirable. Nausiphanes was the first atomist to propose that knowledge was both attainable and desirable, and therefore the first dogmatist.

But, if knowledge was attainable, how could it be attained?

It was Nausiphanes who came up with the original idea for a canon or "measurer," which was made up of three tools for discovering reality—the tripod. We do not know if his canon was identical to Epicurus' canon—which consists of sense perceptions, feelings, and anticipations, and will be explained in a later chapter.

The ultimate goal of philosophy, for Nausiphanes, was cheerfulness. Epicurus chose instead *ataraxia* (imperturbability) as the ultimate end because he had admired Pyrrho's imperturbability even as he was critical of his skepticist doctrine. And so, to Epicurus, truth and certainty are desirable and they also should lead to imperturbability and serenity. The study of the nature of things has, therefore, a purpose: the cultivation of peace of mind and the dispelling of irrational fears that are born of ignorance and superstition.

But the main difference of opinion which Epicurus and his master were unable to reconcile had to do with determinism, against which Epicurus rebelled. This matter was important enough that it led to a hostile parting of ways. Philosophy, in order to be a moral force, had to allow for the freedom of the individual.

And so, like Siddhartha Buddha, Epicurus followed several teachers, drew from their teachings, but in the end came independently to a more accurate view of reality as it is. He also was aware of the practical benefits of the wisdom gained and felt compelled to share his teaching just as Siddhartha Buddha did after attaining nirvana under the bodhi tree, which explains why when he exited his ecstatic state of mind, his hand touched the ground to assert his return to the ground of reality, and he rose and began preaching. The truths that were discovered had the power to awaken compassion for suffering beings. This is also central to missionary Epicureanism, in spite of the claims by Epicurus' enemies that hedonism is a selfish philosophy. To us, encouraging the flourishing of others and teaching them the best and most scientific methods to attain happiness is an act of philanthropy.

Although there is much in Epicureanism which evolved from Democritan atomism, Epicurus claimed to have been mostly a self-taught philosopher and he founded a noble philosophical tradition that bears his name, the details of which you will find in these pages

Epicurus would have been 18, and in Athens completing his military service, when Alexander the Great was killed and his family was exiled to Colophon, in what is now Turkey. He later joined them there and, although we do not hear any significant biographical details during his next decade, it seems fair to imagine that he slowly developed his philosophy through introspection and exchanges with other philosophers.

The Exile from Lesbos and the Lampsacus School

Although Epicurus was a philosopher, he shared some commonalities with many religious figures and prophets, including later reverence as a culture hero, but also a narrative of exile for sake of his teachings similar to the narrative of Rama, of Moses, of Muhammad, and other religious leaders and moral reformers. Many found his scientific and naturalistic approach to reality impious and an affront to the gods and to religion.

The teaching mission of Epicurus began when he was 32 in the island of Lesbos where he met his first disciple, Hermarchus. There, in the gymnasium in the city of Mytilene, he began teaching his own version of atomist physics and, perhaps, ethics. The Platonist and Aristotelian philosophers that were established there were hostile to the new doctrine and he was forced to leave in the year 331 BCE under threat of being accused of impiety, a crime for which Socrates had been sentenced to death.

> *If Athens was the Mecca of this prophet, Lampsacus was his Medina.*
> —William Wallace

He then founded a school in Lampsacus, where he met the majority of his small but devoted following. This included Metrodorus, Polyaenus, Metrodorus' brother Timocrates and his sister Batis, Leonteus and his wife, Themista, Colotes, and Idomeneus. It's safe to assume that by the time he gathered his first core group of disciples, he must have already perfected an ethical system that fulfilled the deep existential needs of his pupils. He was also known to be a great teacher.

It's in Lampsacus that the tradition of writing epistles with a didactic message to be read publicly evolved among the Epicureans. This style was later copied in the Christian New Testament.

The Athenian Garden

At the age of 35, Epicurus returned to Athens in 306 BCE, where he purchased a home for 80 minae and founded his school known as *Ho Kepos* (The Garden), as it was in his own home and garden where he offered his teaching to his disciples and friends.

There, he sought to create a simple yet hospitable and pleasant environment for philosophy. At the entrance of the Garden, a sign read "Stranger, here you do well to tarry; here our highest good is pleasure". Guests were received with warmth and hospitality. They were offered comforts, water and bread.

The majority of ancient Greeks did not consume meat with frequency. We can imagine Epicurus and his devoted disciples enjoying water, bread, other locally available fruits and vegetables, and sometimes his favorite cheese, which was a delicacy to him.

The nicknames that members of the community gave each other, and the fact that there were already familial and marriage bonds between many of them prior to conversion, suggest a high level of familiarity, intimacy and trust among the early Epicurean friends. The elevation of *suavity* (kind speech) to the status of an important virtue within the school suggests that they seem to have had a habit of affectionately engaging each other in philosophical and friendly discourse with kind words. It's possible that part of their training in philosophy and in human values consisted of learning how to properly treat each other as part of a loving, caring community of philosopher friends.

Some of Epicurus' companions were couples who raised their children in the Gardens. Some married each other's siblings, so that the Garden must have felt like a very hospitable extended family. In his last will, Epicurus spoke of his friends who "grew old with me in philosophy," made sure to provide for some of his companions' children who had come of age there, and emancipated his slaves who, according to all the known sources, were treated as part of the family and engaged in philosophy together with free people as equals. No special attention was paid to reminding them of their place. Epicurus' famous affability toward his slaves was later echoed by Philodemus.

It was in Athens, when the school had become formally founded, that the educational curriculum was first developed and the process of proselytising began. It was there that Epicurus most likely instituted the oath on his core tenets among his followers and encouraged them to proclaim their Epicurean identity, celebrate Epicurean feasts, respect Epicurean elders, and seek the association of like-minded philosophers. The Athenian Garden is where his philosophy acquired the aspect of a tradition.

Epicurus taught for the next 37 years and died at the age of 72 from kidney stones. Of his 300 scrolls, only fragments remain. Most of our sources are indirect and sometimes hostile.

Epicurus is, as his name suggests, a spiritual ally to all who seek to apply philosophy to the pursuit of wisdom and happiness. He was among the first to propose the idea of the atom; he recommended wholesome association, celebrated the role that science played in liberating humans from superstition and unnecessary suffering, and even had an early theory of natural selection, one that preceded Darwin by over two millennia and which serves as the foundation for our calculated, philosophical hedonism where desires are kept under control. Epicurus brought the treasure of his science of happiness to thousands of followers who, in a spirit of deep and sincere gratitude, honored him as their founding hero who liberated them from false idols, from misery, and from ignorance.

The Tradition After the Founder

After Epicurus died, three of his associates had gained enough prominence for all four to be considered founding figures and be collectively referred to as "The Men": Metrodorus, Hermarchus, and Polyaenus. Plural leadership goes back to our early beginnings all the way to Epicurus himself who, on his will, instituted the celebrations on the twentieth of every month in memory of both himself and Metrodorus.

During the first century BCE, Syrian philosopher Philodemus of Gaddara is credited with being a prolific writer and teacher of Epicureanism. Some believe that he organized the doctrine into the Four Remedies for didactic purposes, and many of his scrolls were found in the Herculaneum during the twentieth century. They had been burnt by the Mount Vesuvius eruption of the first century, but some of the fragments were somewhat decipherable.

Roman Epicurean poet Lucretius, who lived during the first century BCE, wrote *De Rerum Natura*, or *On the Nature of Things*, an epic poem that included a naturalist and more or less scientific, for his day, account of both biological and social evolution, as well as explanations of how natural phenomena such as lightning and the movements of heavenly bodies are not the work of the gods.

Much of his work was a precocious diatribe against creationism and its modern variant, intelligent design. He argued that fear of the gods was inconsistent with civilized life and sought scientific explanations for natural phenomena. He also provided a lengthy presentation of Epicurean atomism and physics, theology, and other points of the doctrine. His poem remains the most valuable source for ancient Epicurean thought. Stephen Greenblatt (2012) argues that the poem ignited the spark of the Renaissance and Enlightenment.

Another prominent Epicurean was Diogenes of Oenoanda, who lived in what is today known as Turkey during the second century CE. He is famous for having erected a wall in his home town which bore a 25,000 word-long inscription of Epicurean teachings for the benefit of all passers-by. Fragments of his wall remain to this day.

Most other sources are indirect, non-Epicurean and sometimes hostile: stoic philosopher Seneca admired our hegemon so much that he advised people to "Do all things as if Epicurus was watching" (perhaps repeating a teaching of the Epicureans themselves?), an adage which the modern Society of Epicurus adopted as our motto.

On the other hand, Plutarch mocked Colotes for his conversion to Epicureanism, but in doing so provided us indirectly with many of Colotes' arguments for his faith in Epicurus, which he was refuting. The convert's arguments revolved around his belief that, of all the philosophies, the one taught by Epicurus was the only pragmatic one that could really be practiced.

The hospitable, progressive Epicurean schools were oases of tranquility, learning, cultivation of self, and pleasure known as Gardens, where the ideals of civilized friendship flourished and men, women and even slaves engaged in philosophical discourse. They flourished for over 700 years until Emperor Justinian had all the philosophical schools that competed with Christianity closed.

Sadly, only fragments remain of the 300 scrolls that Epicurus wrote. Lucretius' epic poem *On the Nature of Things* was lost to us until in 1417, at the onset of the Renaissance, Poggio Bracciolini rediscovered a manuscript.

After the calamities of the Dark Ages, the philosophy flourished again during the Renaissance and influenced Enlightenment thinkers. Its influence would be evident in the person of Pierre Gassendi, who sought to reconcile Epicurus' materialism and atomism with Christianity, and then from him it would trickle down to Isaac Newton and eventually to other Enlightenment thinkers.

The Jefferson Bible and the Philosophical Roots of the American Dream

"As you say of yourself, I too am an Epicurean!"
—Thomas Jefferson, Letter to William Short

Thomas Jefferson referred to Epicurus as his Master, a fact which explains his belief—enshrined in our Declaration of Independence—that the pursuit of happiness was inherent to human nature and human dignity. We must therefore not underestimate the considerable influence that Epicurus had even in our national narrative, the American Dream.

While Epicurus advised that we should live unknown, Jefferson was engaged in public life and did not shy away from politics. He therefore represents an evolution, or maybe even a reform of Epicurean tradition. Any explanation of how Jefferson lived out his Epicureanism in the spotlight should consider hedonic calculus, which will be discussed at length when we address the moral question of anger and is usually the Epicurean answer to both common and difficult moral questions. What if fame is acquired at the right time in history in the pursuit of other, higher or nobler, values and desires? What if one can manage to live a life of relative imperturbability while engaging in worldly affairs?

Epictetus and Epicurus give laws for governing ourselves, Jesus a supplement of the duties and charities we owe to others.
—Thomas Jefferson

Jefferson also took the gospels and cut off all the supernatural claims, keeping only the ethical teachings and titling his humanist gospel *The Life and Morals of Jesus of Nazareth*. This act constituted a commentary on Jesus born of Epicurean naturalist conviction. He was a philosophical materialist and had no need for the supernatural claims.

The Jefferson Bible is not just the editorial process that, on its face, it seems to be. By cutting off the supernatural (and ergo un-natural) portions, Jefferson was adding valuable, naturalist commentary to the life and ethics of Jesus, and engaging in secular philosophical and ethical discourse. The Jefferson Bible is an expression of the founding father's secular humanist philosophy. He was saying: "These portions are unnecessary and fraudulent, but these others are valuable."

For many of us who have a Christian background, Jefferson's synthesis and dialectical relationship with a humanist version of that other cultural hero of Western civilization, Jesus of Nazareth, whose altruistic teachings he believed counterbalanced the philosophy of Epicurus, represent an attempt to take back Jesus from the Platonists and the religionists and to shed new light on the value of his (and our) humanity. He was claiming Jesus for naturalist philosophers and for Epicureans.

Like Jefferson, many Unitarians and people in other progressive Christian traditions are developing a more sober, philosophical approach to Jesus these days, an approach which for many people feels healthier than a full dismissal of religious tradition. The Jefferson Bible is a symbol of how philosophy can civilize religion and save it from its superstitious roots and from the irrational elements that steal the luster of the wisdom traditions that are often embedded into religious lore.

It must be said that Epicureanism is not necessarily an atheist philosophy although many adherents are atheists. There are agnostics who deny the practical importance, possibility or relevance of belief in gods, as well as deists who

believe that gods exist but that they're completely unconcerned with our natural world. This latter deist belief was Jefferson's (and, for the record, Epicurus') own view.

If we replace the word "God" with the term "nature" in
many of the non-supernatural passages of the gospels, we
will easily understand how a naturalist Christian thinker can
also be an Epicurean. Jesus taught that God (nature) feeds the
birds daily and that this is seen as proof of how we should not
live in fear of the difficulties of finding food. Epicurus also
teaches that that which is necessary for life has been made
easy to procure by nature. Unlike Jesus, we go a step further
and explain that natural selection has made it easy for both
birds and humans to procure their food, but the intent of the
teaching is the same: we must purge our fear of not being able
to attain our basic needs.

In our tradition, it is important to name nature as the
teacher because the implications of this are considerably different from those of religious language. Pleasure is how nature
guides sentient beings to that which helped their ancestors to
survive. It's the suavity in nature's speech. Therefore, we say
that it is not only easy but also pleasant to fulfill our basic
needs.

Jefferson demonstrates that Epicureans and humanists
are not anti-Jesus in spite of our firm rejection of supernatu-
ralism, and also that not all Epicureans reject engagement in
the world: that we are today as diverse and cosmopolitan as
we were in antiquity.

References

Greenblatt, Stephen. *The Swerve: How the World Became Modern.* (New York: W. W. Norton & Company, 2012).
Lucretius Carus, Titus. *De Rerum Natura.* Leonard, William
E. (Trans.). Retrieved from http://classics.mit.edu/Carus/
nature_things.html

Wallace, William. *Epicureanism.* (London: Society for Promoting Christian Knowledge, 1880) Retrieved from http://www.epicurus.info/etexts/wallace_epicureanism.html

III

PLANTING SEEDS FOR A FUTURE HARVEST
The Modern School

If such was the influence of Epicurus in history and in the progression of scientific thought while being nearly invisible, we can only begin to imagine the influence he would have had, had Justinian allowed the philosophical schools to remain open.

For years, I told myself: "Wouldn't it be great if the Epicurean Gardens had remained open, if they were as mainstream today as the churches that we see in every corner?" Then in early 2013, I decided to become the change I want to see and to found the Society of Friends of Epicurus in order to reinstate the teaching mission of the Gardens and to ensure the cultural continuity of Epicureanism.

The Society of Friends of Epicurus seeks to experiment with replicating the ancient therapeutic practice of Epicureanism and to update the tradition in light of centuries of philosophical discourse and scientific insight. This book is, therefore, less about the history of Epicureanism, and more about its new roots and branches, and its eternally relevant truths. We are, again, tending our Gardens.

Gardens cannot exist without gardeners: in the same manner, there were Guides in antiquity who taught and led others through the process of Epicurean therapy. Much of the art of living that the ancients practiced must therefore evolve within a new cultural context, a process which is likely to take many years if new Guides are to be nurtured within the new communities that we create.

Our faith and resolution to follow Epicurus can be understood as a seed. Our species is known as *homo sapiens* because, imprinted within our very identity, is the eternal quest for wisdom, for *sapiens*. We all start out as philosophers in a dormant state. In every Garden there are seedlings which sprout from our faith in philosophy and its consolations, and which must be nurtured if they are to bear the sweet fruits of equanimity, good character, and a pleasant life. Happiness and success, to us, is not measured by how much wealth we amass. We can judge whether or not we are living a wholesome life of philosophy by the quality and pleasantness of our lives.

A philosopher's words are empty if they do not heal the suffering of mankind. For just as medicine is useless if it does not remove sickness from the body, so philosophy is useless if it does not remove suffering from the soul.

—Epicurus

Like the Buddha, Epicurus taught that suffering has an origin, and accurately pointed the finger at our vain and mindless desires as the first place where we must take up spiritual discipline. There are tasks, both introspective and social, that we must carry out if we are to cultivate the art of living an analyzed life in order to purge pain, unpleasantness, and moral disease from our lives, minds and characters. Most of these tasks are universal to all humankind, whereas others may emerge from our personal history and upbringing. Some require less work, while others are an ongoing life-long process.

The ancient Gardens had a teaching mission and were the only missionary secular humanist philosophy to come out of Greece. What this tells us is that the followers found deep fulfillment in Epicureanism and felt an intense desire to share the treasure of a compassionate, therapeutic philosophy that helped people to live happy and wholesome lives.

Epicurus encouraged communities of philosophers who associate with others of like mind and live a tranquil, happy life of wisdom, for he saw that association greatly affects character. Our success ultimately should produce robust branches and fruits within the Garden so that the fragrance of the flowers of a person's good character will intersperse with that of others. The Society of Epicurus therefore seeks to create communities of Philosopher-Friends who derive mutual benefit from wholesome association.

One of the goals of therapeutic philosophy is to produce a sense of *eudaimonia*, which is usually translated as overall happiness and fulfillment, but the more accurate translation of *eudaimonia* is flourishing. Hence, it's possible that Epicurus very consciously chose the metaphor of the Garden for his schools because they were created as spaces where people can flourish and be happy. The metaphor of flourishing reminds me of the lotus flower and of Buddhist and Hindu traditions that use a similar metaphor for spiritual awakening.

It also, importantly, accentuates the deep contrast that exists between Garden spirituality which affirms life and matter/reality versus the desert spirituality of Abrahamic religions which, in my view, is an attempt to escape, to deny life and reality. Although we teach frugality and although both the Garden and the desert are places sought for the sake of insight and self-betterment, we are not deniers of the world who embrace false consolations from the imaginary realm. Our epistemology is founded on the senses and affirms nature and this world with deep conviction. We can only flourish by being grounded and having our feet firmly planted on the ground of reality, which is the aim that the canon serves within our tradition.

The Garden and the idea of flourishing are two of the central spiritual metaphors in our tradition. The moment of flourishing is when the plant is at its most creative, open, alive, fragrant, pleasant, giving its fruits, productive, with all of its dormant potentials fully activated. It reaches its full beauty and potential. An Epicurean Garden, therefore, must be the ideal place for such a flourishing in terms of human potential and perhaps Epicurus himself can be understood as the archetypal Gardener that tends to the existential health of those who entrust themselves to his teaching in order to blossom.

For centuries, Epicureans have been repeatedly accused of selfish hedonism by people with limited understanding of the difference between temperate philosophical hedonism and the vulgar, mindless hedonism and consumerism of the uncultivated masses. The fact is that pleasure can be either selfish or can serve as the lubricant that binds friends, lovers, a mother to her child, etc. It can be both selfish and altruistic at once: we're often pleased to please our friends and loved ones. Pleasure is the suavity in nature's language, nature's way of advising us that we are doing the things that will lead to our survival, which is why pleasant things are always good if we are prudent.

The Society of Friends of Epicurus firmly rejects the notion that pleasure is always and only selfish, and boldly embraces the belief that life should be pleasant. It is a philanthropic and educational organization that seeks to teach humanity how to live a pleasant life through the practice of applied philosophy.

Defining the Ideal of Ataraxia

Having imbibed the flavor of solitude and the flavor of tranquility, one becomes free from fear and free from evil, drinking the juice of delight in Truth.
—Dhammapada 15:9

Before we begin to acquaint ourselves with the practicalities of the work that we do as Epicureans, we must set a goal and clearly determine a purpose and a context for our practice. *Ataraxia* is the Greek word for imperturbability. It generally translates as tranquility or equanimity, and it's the *telos* or the goal of all wholesome ethical philosophy. Pleasure is our ultimate goal, but it's defined in terms of not having perturbances. Therefore, pleasure and *ataraxia* are treated as one and the same. The entire system of Epicurus' teachings is meant to cultivate this quality, which makes perturbation (defined as mental disquiet, disturbance, or agitation) the enemy of the philosopher.

Like Buddha's doctrine on *nirvana*, the stability of ataraxia requires the extinction of desires, to reach a state of satisfaction, of not-wanting and not-hungering, but it is an entirely secular, naturalist philosophical ideal. Epicurus, however, did not shun all desire. He was a pragmatist who distinguished between the necessary and the unnecessary desires, and concluded that since we cannot escape certain needs (such as shelter, human association, or food), the wise man should cheerfully attend to the necessary desires and dismiss the unnecessary and vain desires. He also pointed to the fact that these needs are easy to procure.

> *Our longing, our craving, our thirsting for something other*
> *than Reality is what dissatisfies us.*
> —Steve Hagen

Desires are like fire. When fed, they get stronger and they want more. When we indulge in them, we find that they increase over time instead of going away. They can also become addictive and enslave us. Research indicates that sugar is as addictive as any other drug and that when people fall in love, the brain operates as if addicted to another person. We must therefore make a very careful choice when we accept a dependable lover. We can easily become dependent on externals and must therefore be ever watchful of our minds.

Ataraxia is satisfaction with life as it is here and now, not seeking its perfection but accepting its limitations and never minding them. It's the mental "aboveness" of one who's learned to be happy and to live in a pleasant state always, regardless of conditions. Ataraxia is unconditional pleasure in living and the good news is that there are methods to cultivate it.

This does not mean that the philosopher is easily defeated in life and merely rolls with the punches. A wise person prudently sets goals, is diligent, and achieves them. In fact, autarchy or self-sufficiency is one of the three goods within Epicurus' doctrine, perhaps the most worldly of them. There is a distinction between going after desirable things in life and needing them for our happiness. We can go after those things with detachment, without our moods ever being affected by the results of our obligations and efforts. This is an important part of the Epicurean art of living the good life.

Gratitude, Recollection and Oblivion

Many methods have been used by Epicureans to cultivate the stability of ataraxia. One of the remedies that Epicurus employed was recollection, which must hold hands with oblivion. He recognized that we are all selective in our memory, that impressions of past pleasures stay in the mind and can be evoked easily. This includes fond memories of laughter and play with friends, of the affection of loved ones, of happy songs, funny situations, and silly people. The creation of fond memories becomes easier when we have good friends.

Epicurus in his death bed, on his last day on earth and while experiencing great physical pain, wrote an epistle to a friend where he confessed how happy he was to reminisce about their time together. Being able to easily ignore pain and to evoke and hold pleasant recollections is an art that can be learned.

The ingratitude of the soul makes a creature greedy for endless variation in its way of life.
—Vatican Sayings, 69

Equally important is gratitude, which might be seen as a form of recollection of the good things that we sometimes take for granted. Sincere gratitude is an act of instant awakening which changes any situation into a positive one. There are studies that suggest a clear positive correlation between gratitude and happiness (Tierney, 2011).

When we delve into the specifics of Epicurus' theory of happiness and discuss the importance of abiding pleasures, it will become evident that daily gratitude is one of the most fundamental and easy to practice among the "katastemic" disciplines (that is, those related to the cultivation of abiding pleasure). A daily gratitude journal entry or contemplation, a simple act of mindful recognition of the things one is grateful for, greatly aids in the cultivation of a happy mind.

Recollection should be balanced with oblivion: the blessed ability to forget unpleasant situations and people. Loved ones who pass away or move on should be let go after our initial mourning. This is healing after the trauma of death or separation. Sad or difficult situations should also be let go. A philosopher must learn the art of dismissal, along with the art of recollection.

When we've been wronged, we often tell ourselves we'll never forget. But do we really want to never forget? Do we really wish to live our short years regretting what could have been, or nurturing our grief and hatred? Is it intelligent to make ourselves miserable while living in the past, haunted by memories while being inexorably swallowed by time? That is a choice we have to make frequently. Whenever we reminisce about our past life, we are advised in our tradition to be in a state of gratefulness. Be mindful of nurturing unnecessary grief and staying stuck in old pain.

The value of forgetfulness is one of the most important principles in the science of happiness. The inability to let go can be a painful disease and should be treated like an enemy who has wronged us for years.

If by bad habit our minds frequently evoke a memory or an experience of anger, fear or other negative experiences, one technique is to choose a word that we can train ourselves to use to instantly and confidently dismiss them. Buddhists do this with the word *neti*, which translates as "not this," or "not now." In Epicurean parlance, these techniques are known as remedies (from the Greek *pharmakon*).

There is a reason why nature has stipulated that we must have a cycle of sleep and wakefulness. The mind needs to reboot, recharge, and begin again. Otherwise, it gets saturated with experience and we're exhausted.

Thankfully, every morning we live again, and we have this choice to recollect and forget at every moment. This is one way in which ataraxia is cultivated.

The Three Goods

A good is anything that is sought because it has inherent value in itself, not for the sake of attaining other things. Most virtues are considered higher goods. In Epicurean doctrine there are three main goods. Because the goal of life is pleasure, it is understood that it's impossible to have a pleasant life without them and that, therefore, they should be thought of as non-different from pleasure.

1. Analyzed Life
2. Friendship
3. Autarchy

The Analyzed Life

The unexamined life is not worth living —Socrates

Self examination was so important to ancient Greeks that at the great temple in Delphi, there was an inscription that said "Know Thyself," and this was embraced as one of the central adages of philosophy. There are many dangers associated with not knowing ourselves, but the one that concerns us Epicureans the most is the vast amount of unnecessary suffering that arises from consensus, ignorance and irrational fears.

In order to fulfill societal norms, superstitious beliefs that people dare not question, or religious obligations, there are those who torture their children, who force or influence people to marry someone they don't love against their will, to work at a job where they're miserable, to hate gays, to not speak up against abuse for fear of authority, to treat women like children and deny them fundamental civil rights like the right to drive a car or choose a husband, etc. There is no rational foundation for much of the habitual behavior of people in many cultures. The lack of analysis becomes more pernicious, the more we ponder how much suffering it generates.

But those are the most obvious examples. What about a man's eternal infatuation with the wrong person? Or a woman's inability to leave an abusive relationship based on lack of self-confidence and belief that she must "bear her cross," or to embrace a wholesome one based on fears that were learned as a child? What about how sleeping in a certain position produces chronic pain in the back or elbows for some people ... who won't sleep any other way? Or how eating certain foods produces migraines, but some people keep eating them?

The law of inertia is everywhere. We are all habitual persons, but if we become cognizant of these customs, we can start implementing methods to remove the weeds of bad habits and to nurture the roots of good habits. If we examine our lives frequently, we can evaluate whether our efforts are actually working, or if other, more effective methods need to be implemented. Success in life invariably requires leaving behind bad habits and developing new habits and ways of thinking. This takes time and effort.

If we wish to experience a happier life, we must examine it daily, watch our moods, the effects of different foods and people in our minds, the impressions we carry from past experiences that unfairly influence our current decisions and relations, the habits that we take for granted until our bodies, our minds, or other people make us aware of them.

We also cannot cultivate a good character, discern between vice and virtue, or have any sense of ethics, without living an examined life. Only by mindfulness can we understand intuitively and rationally the ways in which living a pleasant life makes us more productive and happier, and makes those around us happier; or the ways in which anger, hate, and violence lead to a hellish existence; or the ways in which feeling compassion for an enemy is actually easier and less taxing than hating him. We also cannot properly conduct hedonic calculus—the comparative evaluation of the pleasure and pain generated by a decision or action—without analyzing our lives.

We often rationalize our negative emotions because we've been hurt, entering cycles of pain that can be stopped by intelligently cultivating new habits and paying attention to more wholesome things.

Attention is the tool that our minds use to create our reality: if we let it slide on forever like a river, we'll get lost in the crevices of inertia and habit. By consciously choosing to live up to our resolution to live a good life, and by paying attention to our own nature, we ensure that we are the ones who steer the boat, not our unconscious tendencies.

New Verbiage:

Ataraxia
Good
Gratitude Journal
Hedonic Calculus

Task: Journaling and Other Methods of Introspection

You will derive the most benefits from the book you're reading if you journal or blog frequently about its contents. You may also have a daily period of introspection, perhaps right before bed every night, to consider the main events of the day and what you can learn from them.

Use journaling not just to assimilate, ponder, and recognize what you're learning, but also to set goals and to periodically touch base with yourself regarding them. These can be as simple as avoiding the use of a certain word or song that perturbs the mind, or avoiding a certain bad association or bad habit. This method is very easy to implement and considered by many to be one of life's simple pleasures.

Use journaling also in your life-long process of creating meaning and value and for training yourself as a philosopher. You may even engage in a process of reasoning with Epicurus, having a dialectical relationship with his ideas in order to assimilate them through journaling. The lack of the 300 scrolls Epicurus wrote should, ideally, serve as an encouragement for us to develop a vibrant literary tradition by writing another 300 works in honor of his memory!

Task: State your Resolution to Apply Epicureanism

You may or may not officially adopt an Epicurean outlook after you read this book, but you will derive the most benefit from it if you sincerely immerse yourself in the teachings of Epicurus at least for a period in your life. Develop a resolve to follow Epicurus and study his teachings for three months at least. You may want to adapt Philodemus' oath for this: "I will be faithful to Epicurus according to whom it has been my choice to live ... this month."

This will allow you time to begin to find the voice of your inner philosopher, to experience Epicureanism from within as an adherent, to evaluate and either challenge or enhance your own beliefs and values, and to implement your hedonic regimen and your long-term plan for autarchy (self-sufficiency).

It will give you time to introspect about your autarchy, your own authority, and about what you want to do with all the freedom that you were born with; to begin to nurture your inner autarch, your inner philosophical hero. This is an extremely important task. You'll find that a philosophy of freedom is, necessarily, a creative wisdom tradition and one that, ideally, leads to huge responsibility and overall success in life—measured, of course, by standards that must also be carefully and intelligently analyzed. This book, if anything, should inspire you to begin or revisit your assessment of your short-term and long-term existential, fiscal, introspective and relational projects.

Therefore, it requires a resolution or an agreement with yourself, which you may decide to write down on a piece of paper, to follow through on whatever valuable insights you gain from it. Resolve to turn the Epicurean learning experience into one of your projects this year by dedicating several months of your life to introspecting sincerely on this book and wherever it leads you. Whether or not you end up calling yourself an Epicurean, you will grow as a person if you do so.

References:

Hagen, Steve. *Buddhism Plain and Simple*. (New York: Broadway Books, 1998).

Tierney, John. "A Serving of Gratitude May Save the Day." *The New York Times*, November 21, 2011. Retrieved from http://www.nytimes.com/2011/11/22/science/a-serving-of-gratitude-brings-healthy-dividends.html?_r=0

IV

THE FOUR REMEDIES

Do not fear the gods
Do not fear death
What is good is easy to attain
What is bad is easy to endure

Tetrapharmakon (Four Cures)

The Tetrapharmakon, our basic four prescriptions for human life, are by no means the only remedies in the pharmacology of Epicurus, but they are the most universal and comprise the basic premises of the doctrine from which the rest of the teaching flows.

Do Not Fear: Epicurus is Here

There are several naturalist explanations for the near universality of worship. The father of psychoanalysis, Carl Jung, proposed that people have inherited instincts just as they have inherited physical traits and that the gods are archetypes of the collective unconscious, inherited conceptions and behaviors tied to our evolutionary and psychological history.

Dr. Daisy Grewal, a researcher at the Stanford School of Medicine, recently published the results of a study on anti-atheist prejudice in *Scientific American* where she concluded that "reminding people about God's presence has the same effect as telling people they are being watched by others: it increases their feelings of self-consciousness and leads them to behave in more socially acceptable ways." She found epidemic levels of distrust of atheists, but also discovered that people were more able to trust atheists when they were reminded of authority figures like judges and police chiefs.

In other words, any divine or secular authority figure will do, and it's the authority vacuum that feels uncomfortable for many people.

There are probably many reasons for the near universality of belief in, and fear of, spirits and gods. From time immemorial, human beings have lived in fear of natural, unexplained, and awesome phenomena. To a pre-scientific person, the experience of a tsunami or an earthquake was a sign of the anger of Poseidon or some other deity. Volcanoes also conjured up angry war deities. Thunder and lightning were the domain of the alpha male in the sky, Zeus.

Humanity has not overcome the primitive tendency to relate nature phenomena, or even man-made warfare, to whimsical or impulsive spiritual beings. There are still religious leaders who attribute geological and weather phenomena to the gods: people with certain political agendas claimed that hurricane Katrina was caused by the wrath of God at people's tolerance of gays and at liberals. Many victims of the HIV epidemic are blamed for their woes, as were Haitians after the 2010 earthquake. If, in the future, the city of Miami sinks under the waves as a result of rising sea levels, surely someone will claim it's because of the prevalence of animal sacrifice among practitioners of Santeria and Voodoo there (never mind Leviticus). Value judgments of this kind say more about whoever is doing the judging than about those being misjudged: we get to see their true intentions, animosities, bigotry and ill-will. The behavior and expression of those who still believe in wrathful deities is often laughably credulous and reveals the nakedness of their latent tyranny.

Epicurus offers us instead a taboo against fearing the gods as the first of four remedies to begin our emancipation from superstition and to begin reaping the benefits of applied philosophy. This remedy calls for the development of a scientific understanding of nature. Science, in Epicureanism, is the first of our consolations.

If our suspicions about astronomical phenomena and about death were nothing to us and troubled us not at all, and if this were also the case regarding our ignorance about the limits of our pains and desires, then we would have no need for studying what is natural. It is impossible for someone who is completely ignorant about nature to wash away his fears about the most important matters if he retains some suspicions about the myths. So it is impossible to experience undiluted enjoyment without studying what is natural. It is useless to be safe from other people while retaining suspicions about what is above and below the earth and in general about the infinite unknown.

—Principal Doctrines 11-13

Many atheists claim Epicurus as one of them and say that he did not come out as atheist because he feared he might suffer the same fate as Socrates. Or perhaps he was a kind atheist who did not want to insult the sincere beliefs of his peers. But Epicurus never dismissed the gods: he seems to have been, like Thomas Jefferson, a deist who thought they were unconcerned with human problems and that ethics was the province of humans, not of the gods.

Epicurus thought that religion, for all its art and poetry, also has its dangers and that civilized man must protect himself and his mind from these dangers. He was a humanist who saw our dependence on the gods as infantile and as a force that keeps us from effectively creating the beautiful lives of dignity that we are all worthy of.

It is foolish to ask of the gods that which we can supply for ourselves.

—Vatican Saying 65

Oftentimes we fear the gods because we have wrong beliefs about the ways in which they take an interest in our world: we may think they're punitive or have intentions and plans that we mortals may or may not have the power to thwart. But we may also fear the gods out of expectation and as a result of the belief that they answer our prayers, or that if we don't pray for something we won't get it, or that only if we behave a certain way will we get an answer to our prayers.

The general belief that gods concern themselves with mortals is at the root of all these fears and neuroses. In Epicurean therapy, these anxieties are healed when we fully develop a conviction in the non-involvement of the gods. Some of the remedies that Epicureans have traditionally used to develop this conviction have included memorization and repetition of Epicurean teachings.

Another way to develop this conviction is to engage in argument against the specific fears or expectations we hold. If we believe in divine punishment, we may consider the ways in which sexual predators, murderers, and thieves have gotten away with their crimes, usually because of their wealth, their wit, their allegiances or other privileges, as well as the ways in which good and innocent people have suffered tremendously in spite of their good character.

As we develop a resolve to be happy, we must not expect the world to be fair or just and we must know that it's unintelligent for fairness to be a condition of our happiness. Our happiness, our tranquility, must not depend on groundless expectations. We must develop the confidence that we can be happy regardless of life's highs and lows, even as we do our part to create a more just world.

If we have come to believe that we won't make a good living without the auspices of God or the gods, then we should think of all the atheists who have led successful lives, of the fact that 93 percent of the members of the Academy of the Sciences are atheists, or perhaps study atheist prison, divorce, and other such statistics. We may also consider the idea that people of diverse religions enjoy wealth and poverty: there are rich oil investors in Saudi Arabia who are Muslim, but there are some in Texas who are Christian, and while some of the wealthiest and happiest countries are atheist societies in Scandinavia, there are also wealthy states in the Middle East, Asia and elsewhere in Europe and the Americas. To fear the god of any particular religion in expectation of material returns is to act based on groundless expectations and false opinion.

One obstacle to the development of humanist faith (that is, faith in our humanity and in human values rather than religious values) exists among men who feel that they cannot be faithful to their wives, or people who feel they cannot stop using drugs, alcohol, or abandon certain bad habits, without the help of a higher power of some kind. This is because their notion of a higher power is tied to societal and familial expectations and with the experience of shame, as much as it is tied to the experience of being loved and strengthened within the context of familiar religious traditions: a powerful psychological dynamo. Some of us may argue that it's probably best for people with weak stamina of character to stay religious if they cannot control their passions.

This, however, speaks volumes about the problems of which religion may be a symptom. In fact, prison and other statistics, as they relate to levels of religiosity, shed much light on this (Paul, 2005). As far as Epicurean teaching is concerned, we must always protect our minds, and the use of religious belief in therapy is not in itself harmful as long as people do not exhibit neurotic fears and expectations or give up their autonomy and responsibility by enslaving themselves to unwholesome ideologies. For instance, the aesthetically pleasing contemplation of divine imperturbability that is experienced in the chanting of Hindu *bhajans*, or in some forms of Buddhist meditation, do not seem harmful to our imperturbability.

In other words, it's fear-based religion and religion that derives its values from death (as if it was anything other than non-being) rather than life that are taboo for us. Many celebratory, cultural, devotional and ethical aspects of traditional religion are not in themselves dangerous. The Epicurean philosopher lives an analyzed life and attempts to be in tune with the underlying psychological drama in order to become competent at resolving inner difficulties through the process of introspection.

Death: A Naturalist Approach

The second remedy, "Do not fear death," is not too different in rationale from the first, and here again a scientific understanding of the nature of death is needed. Epicurus accurately explained that the atoms in our body simply return to the elements.

We now have the beginnings of a science of death. Recent studies of the phenomenon of near-death experiences (NDE) demonstrate that these experiences are linked to oxygen depletion. When the brain stops receiving oxygen and gets the message that inevitable death is near, the brain stops spending energy on our fight-or-flight instinct and other survival mechanisms and begins to produce ecstatic and visionary experiences. Our body and soul, it turns out, have the wisdom to know how to die with dignity and relative painlessness.

When the creature who is dying has no hope of survival, the stress hormones required to survive are no longer deemed necessary and the brain produces its final medicine: the sweet and blissful escape of psychoactive hormones. The god of death Dionysus is, after all, also the god of ecstasy.

The Death Denial Principle

The death denial principle—introduced by Ernest Becker in a 1973 book—proposes that humans try to escape the anxiety, fear, and panic inspired by their own mortality by escaping into fantasies about immortality. The principle explains not just religious fantasies about the afterlife, but many expressions of art, culture, and funerary traditions.

More recently, follow-up research by social scientists on the death-denial principle demonstrates that, when reminded of their own mortality, judges give more severe penalties and people become judgmental and hostile towards those that are different and attach themselves to that which is familiar. Similar hostilities are exhibited by people who have beliefs about the afterlife when they encounter those who reject their particular beliefs: studies demonstrate that, when reminded of their own mortality, Christians will increase their hostility towards Jews or atheists for rejecting faith in Jesus, which is tied to their particular afterlife fantasies. The death denial principle explains many of the religious prejudices that plague us and sheds light on unending religious conflicts such as the one we see in Israel. Fear of death, particularly when exacerbated by frequent reminders of it, produces ethnic and religious enmity.

Death denial research should serve as a warning against the unanalyzed life and as an argument for applied philosophy. Not only do we subject ourselves to unscrupulous religious leaders who prey on human vulnerabilities when we fear death and fail to understand it as a completely natural phenomenon that can be scientifically approached rather than a supernatural one, but we also may unknowingly feed our prejudices and act out unconscious hostilities.

Although reason and cognitive therapy seem harsh in their treatment of death, and seem disconnected with the visceral and unconscious mechanisms that keep us fearful and vulnerable before death, we should consider that worrying and being anxious about it does not change the fact of death. In the end, we all die anyway. Our final vulnerability is not reduced by our fantasies about a needless, arrogant desire for immortality. We must learn to honor the memory and the dignity of our loved ones and of our own lifespan, and learn to love, enjoy and value our temporary existence, while accurately perceiving the nature of death and our natural limits.

Applying Epicurean Cognitive Therapy to Fear of Death

The argument that Epicurus proposed to tackle fear of death, produced from a hedonist perspective, was concisely presented in his letter to Menoeceus:

Accustom yourself to believing that death is nothing to us, for good and evil imply the capacity for sensation, and death is the privation of all sentience; therefore a correct understanding that death is nothing to us makes the mortality of life enjoyable, not by adding to life a limitless time, but by taking away the yearning after immortality ...
Foolish, therefore, is the man who says that he fears death, not because it will pain when it comes, but because it pains in the prospect. Whatever causes no annoyance when it is present, causes only a groundless pain in the expectation.
Death, therefore, the most awful of evils, is nothing to us, seeing that, when we are, death is not come, and, when death is come, we are not. It is nothing, then, either to the living or to the dead, for with the living it is not and the dead exist no longer.
But in the world, at one time men shun death as the greatest of all evils, and at another time choose it as a respite from the evils in life. The wise man does not deprecate life nor does he fear the cessation of life.

The argument is that if we are not there to feel pain, there is no pain and no subject to feel it. Fear of death is fear of nothing. There is no-thing to fear, no experience, no person experiencing death. Any fear we have of death is an expectation of a future event which we will never truly witness because we won't be there when it happens.

The second and third arguments against fear of death used in our tradition were articulated by Lucretius. There is the symmetry argument, which says that the time after our death is similar to the time before our birth when nothing was known or experienced. Even if we were to reincarnate, we still would have no memory of the time prior to birth. Why fear it? It is as unintelligent to be needlessly tormented about the afterlife as it is to be tormented about the state prior to birth. Hindu scriptures, although they affirm an afterlife, also contain the consolation of a version of the symmetry argument.

All created beings are unmanifest in their beginning, manifest in their interim state, and unmanifest again when they are annihilated. So what need is there for lamentation?
—Bhagavad Gita 2:28

In our third argument, from the third book of *On the Nature of Things*, Lucretius compares death to sleep and argues that just as we don't fear sleep so we shouldn't fear death.

Nobody misses himself or the life he leads
when both his mind and body have fallen asleep:
For all we care that sleep might be everlasting,
there is no trace of any regret for ourselves:
And yet in sleep the elements have not left us
or wandered away from contact with the senses
and when the man awakes he collects himself.
Death must therefore concern us less than sleep
if anything can be less than nothing is.
Much greater confusion in the material elements
follows at death, and nobody wakes again
when once the chilling interval has occurred.

Another useful remedy for fear of death is used in Buddhist and Tantric traditions where practitioners frequently contemplate the reality of death as a spiritual exercise. The more we encounter death of loved ones and strangers, the more natural and acceptable death becomes to us. We learn to be relatively at ease with death as a natural part of reality. Although not particularly pleasant, there is some therapeutic merit to the practice of attending funerals and contemplating the reality of death. The morbid details of plague, pestilence, and death during the Peloponnesian War in Athens is one instance of Epicurean contemplation on suffering and death which can be found in the concluding book of *On the Nature of Things*.

Contemplating the universality of death brings us to the realization of compassion, for we are all in the same boat. We can only know compassion, defined as shared emotion and empathy, if we have experienced similar suffering and pain as the other. Because anxiety and suffering over death unites all human beings, it becomes an opportunity for developing the most universal variety of compassion born of deep insight.

Here is another instance where virtues can be derived from observing and studying the nature of things. Science and education are not needed to mediate this process. It does not matter whether we are illiterate, educated, young, old, gay, straight, men, women. We the people of all races and ethnicities both religious and non-religious: we are all finite, we are all mortals. Here, we can all be together and know the visceral communion that death imparts on us mortals. As the Mayan proverb says, "I am another you, you are another me."

A side note must be added concerning the fear of an early death and the fear of not completing major tasks or projects that one cherishes. Some Epicureans (including Philodemus) have expressed that early death is unfortunate and that fear of premature death is a natural and unnecessary fear. The reason for considering this form of death as unfortunate has to do with the inability to attain the necessary wisdom to be able to nourish a state of ataraxia. Since ataraxia is the ultimate goal in life and the height of natural pleasure, and since it is assumed that a certain amount of training and cultivation is required to attain it and that this requires a bit of time, then a premature death is considered unfortunate whereas one in old age allows the person to reach a sense of completion and ataraxia. Having said that, some intelligent young people are able to easily attain the heights of wisdom and ataraxia early in life and to die having lived well.

All these teachings are fine. They are rational and common sense. But for some people, they are not enough. What is missing, I believe, is a recognition of the fact that it is impossible to replicate the peace and conviction that Epicurus gave humanity without the communal component of Epicureanism. In other words, it wasn't just the teachings, but the manner in which they were imparted that served as a consolation.

However much we may seek to ignore our vulnerabilities, we must not ignore that we're social entities and that people need people. It is one thing to read these teachings and to study them from a book, but it is quite another thing to have a dear friend, a trusted well-wisher, embrace you and tell you that death is nothing to us; that we're all on the same boat. Friends make all the difference. The experience of these teachings is much more comforting when the proper communal context is added.

It is for this reason that Epicurean therapy can only be fully and accurately experienced within the context of a loving community of like-minded friends and the construction of this network of friends must be understood as one of the most important life-long tasks of every Epicurean philosopher.

Remembrance and Gratitude

The good Epicurean should deliberately focus his attention on past pleasures in order to round off his mental survey of life and die content.
—Voula Tsouna

The recollection of happy memories and the practice of gratitude are used in the Epicurean lifestyle as a way to cultivate abiding pleasure. They can also be specifically applied to our apprehensions about death. In fact, Epicurus himself in his deathbed wrote a letter to a friend detailing how happy he was, in spite of his physical pain, when he remembered the philosophical conversations they had enjoyed.

Rather than anticipate suffering, we are encouraged to train our minds in the practice of recollection of fond memories and in the practice of gratitude so that these practices may serve us at the time of illness, difficulties and agony. We must allow these healthy attitudes and habits to become part of our character and of our very being.

On the Importance of Naturalist Philosophical Conviction

Epicurus appears to have recognized the existence of the unconscious and taught that, through repetition and memorization, the teaching becomes powerful in our soul. A scientific and naturalist understanding of death, coupled with the application of cognitive therapy and the association of like-minded friends, while important, constitute only part of how the teaching becomes powerful.

We must ponder what it means for the teaching to become powerful by considering the process of Epicurean conversion, therapy and re-education as a whole. By converting to a humanist faith, we initiate the adventure of undergoing an inner revolution. Fantasies about the afterlife have such prominence in the culture that, even against naturalist and scientific evidence and in spite of the fact that all religions have mutually contradictory claims about the hypothesized afterlife, they are still granted the privilege of normalcy.

Faith is a word that has been historically misused and is defined as the philosophical virtue of trusting a bona-fide friend or an evidence-based true doctrine, not as credulity in spite of evidence. This philosophical faith, this trust in nature and in Epicurean naturalist philosophy, is considered a virtue. Epicurus promised Menoeceus that if we develop a firm identity and conviction in our naturalist faith, we would live as gods among mortals.

*Exercise yourself in these and related precepts day and night,
both by yourself and with one who is like-minded; then never,
either in waking or in dream, will you be disturbed, but will
live as a God among men. For man loses all semblance of mortality by living in the midst of immortal blessings.*

—Epicurus, in his Epistle to Menoeceus

Epicureanism would not have lasted 700 years as a living
tradition if the practitioners had not reaped the benefits that
Epicurus promised: it is possible that, when faced with people
who were either religious or who had not tended their philosophical Gardens and went through life assaulted by neuroses and irrational fears about the afterlife, the fearless ancient
Epicureans may have felt like they were living as gods among
mortals.

Our tradition teaches that learning how to live and learning how to die are one and the same thing: the art of living
includes the art of dying because we only experience death
while we're alive, as an unfounded fear in anticipation of non-
being. It was Philodemus who said that an Epicurean will live
his life already prepared for burial. Ancient Roman Epicureans had the following words inscribed on their gravestones:
Non fui, fui, non sum, non curo. They translate as "I was not; I
was; I am not; I do not care".

We become aware of the benefits of having our feet firmly
planted on the ground, where we make our Garden, when we
observe that everyone else is dreaming of an escape to other-
worldly lives.

As naturalists, we become aware of the benefits of creating
a pleasant life here and now when we observe that everyone
else is just waiting to die and dreams of pleasures after this life,
never seizing the day, never living fully.

We are happy to approach life with the sober mind of an
Epicurean. Who needs the privilege of consensus? We have
freedom, tranquility and clarity of mind. We should therefore

feel blessed and honored that we received and profited from the message given to us by the well-wisher of humanity.

The Practice of Repetition

In applying the Epicurean method of therapeutic repetition and memorization to our fear and apprehension of death, one example of a mantra from our sources that can be used is any variation of what follows:

death is nothing to us
death is no thing to us
death is not a thing to us
death is non being
death is non reality
ergo death is no thing to us

As this practice is carried out with focus and intention, insight will develop and strengthen its unconscious hold, becoming progressively more powerful. In the case of this mantra, the ultimate realization deals with the fact that only life and reality exist, that non-existence, non-being is not real and, therefore, not a thing. In other words: death is not. Life is.

Plants must have deep roots in order to feed properly from the soil, and they must always seek the light of the sun in order to feed properly through photosynthesis. Similarly, we may think of this process of repetition and memorization, and of the teaching becoming strong in our souls, as watering the root. The process of learning and imbibing the teachings is the other way in which we tend the Garden, akin to seeking the light of the sun. It is through arguments and reasonings that we grow: we must argue against our acquired false beliefs and nurture the teaching.

Good News About the Good Life

The third remedy says that good things are easy to attain. However, one of the first tasks that an ethical philosopher must accomplish is to properly identify the good life. Epicurus taught that the good life is the pleasant life: it's a life of simple pleasures. He defined these pleasures broadly. Any science of happiness must address what the pleasant life feels like, what it consists of and how it is cultivated.

Notice that I do not necessarily treat pleasure as a goal in the manner in which philosophers speak of the *telos*, the aim or ultimate goal in life. This is because research by Matt Killingsworth, from Harvard University, indicates that we are happiest when we are not seeking happiness, but rapt in the moment. Happiness requires focus and is a mode of being, not a mode of seeking. The moment we make the observation that we are happy, we are distancing and isolating ourselves from the experience by the very act of observing, and if we were rapt in musical ecstasy before, now the experience is no longer as ecstatic. The bubble is burst.

The philosophically-hedonistic theory that Epicurus proposed (as opposed to the unbridled hedonism that is practiced by many today, which is *not* Epicurean) calls for a preliminary process of introspection, of discerning between necessary and unnecessary desires. Epicurus recognized that desires, if undisciplined, could become a source of perturbance, pain and confusion and that when men were slaves to their vain whims, they were unhappy. A little wine is good for the heart, but too much wine leaves you dehydrated the following day. A little food is good for the body, but too much food taxes the body. With sex also, as with all other pleasures, when we overindulge, we cease to enjoy the object of pleasure as much. It is impossible to live a pleasant life without understanding how philosophical hedonism differs from mindless hedonism.

Natural wealth is both limited and easy to acquire, but the riches incited by groundless opinion have no end.
—Epicurus' Fifteenth Principal Doctrine

The good news about the pleasant life is that it is very simple and easy to attain. In life, Epicurus taught, we have few real needs—we must eat and drink, we need the protection and safety of shelter, we need both solitude and boundaries, as well as the association of others—and the satisfaction of those few needs can be turned into a healthy and varied regimen of simple pleasures.

We don't need too much food or a huge apartment to be content. It's unintelligent to constantly succumb to craving for more than what we need, or specifically for things that we don't have immediate access to (a filet mignon, a mansion), when we could easily satisfy our needs with other things that are right under our nose (a quick and easy-to-make grilled cheese sandwich, a quiet but cozy studio). We don't need the mansion or the filet mignon. We simply crave them. This is not to say that it is evil to have these things from time to time, but it is unintelligent to depend on them for happiness and it is wise to abide in the confidence that we will be perfectly happy without them.

Contemporary frivolous consumerism is fueled by such constant craving and leads not only to psychological slavery, but also to fiscal slavery. People get into debt in order to live a lifestyle of instant gratification and then spend years paying it back, only to have nothing to show for it at the end of their period of indented slavery. An intelligent person chooses, instead, a life of autarchy, of mental and fiscal independence.

Thomas and Danko (2010) conducted research on the values and behavioral patterns of first-generation millionaires: people who built a fortune without a huge inheritance. The very first similarity that they found between these first-generation millionaires was that they lived below their means.

They cared more about their financial independence than about being ostentatious about their wealth and keeping up with the Joneses.

The greatest fruit of self-reliance is freedom.
—Vatican Saying 77

The 2008 fiscal crisis forced many to unwillingly go frugal and popularized frugality and simple living as a conscious lifestyle. If we're unwillingly frugal, it might help our morale to know that those who have done research on the proven ways to become wealthy know that the choice to live a frugal lifestyle is actually the most common, proven, slow-and-steady path to financial stability and long-term affluence—and that people who look wealthy are often in debt whereas people who are truly wealthy look like the guy next door.

Another Princeton University study demonstrates that there can be a correlation between happiness and wealth for people earning up to $75,000 per year (Kahneman, 2010). Income over that figure does not affect happiness: the correlation between wealth and happiness reaches its plateau there. On the other hand, low income does make experiences like divorce and poverty more tragic and painful, and ergo poverty should not be idealized or sought as an alternative. There are many anecdotes about entire societies who live in poverty and live an exuberantly happy, simple life thanks to a strong sense of community and wholesome cultural values. The key is, then, to be able to discern what is truly necessary and important, and then to have enough of it.

Ergo, just as Epicurus said "we need not the appearance of health but true health," the same must be said of wealth. Let's not be manipulated by appearances.

The desires that do not bring pain when they go unfulfilled are not necessary; indeed they are easy to reject if they

are hard to achieve or if they seem to produce harm.
—Principal Doctrine 26

Epicurus categorized desires as necessary or unnecessary. He also discerned between dynamic (*kinetic*) versus abiding (*katastemic*) pleasures. That is, active pleasures (those that are experienced when we engage and participate in an activity) versus passive pleasures (those that derive from satiation and absence of pain).

The pleasures we experience when we enjoy games and sports, consume food or drinks, have sex, and so on, are dynamic. These should be part of our regimen of pleasures. But Epicurus also held the view that a wise person learns to cultivate a pleasant mind and pleasant moods independent of external conditions and that, therefore, there is in philosophy the higher, more stable category of abiding pleasure. If we train ourselves daily to experience abiding pleasure, imperturbability will naturally become part of our demeanor. Abiding pleasure is immortal and godlike, not transient.

In other words, a mindful philosopher understands that when there is no pain, nothing to complain about, no desires, this is an auspicious time and that there's reason to be happy. One simple remedy to assist us in developing a state of abiding pleasure so that we can graduate to the stability of ataraxia is to cultivate an attitude of gratitude.

Misfortune must be cured through gratitude for what has been lost and the knowledge that it is impossible to change what has happened.
—Vatican Saying 55

Daniel Gilbert (2007), a Harvard psychologist who has conducted research on the science of happiness, proposes a theory of happiness that confirms the teachings of Epicurus, even if he uses different verbiage. What our Hegemon calls abiding (katastemic) pleasure, he calls synthetic happiness, which he defines as the happiness we experience when we don't get what we want. He contrasts this against natural happiness, which we experience when we get what we want (kinetic pleasure).

Because synthetic happiness requires no externals, it is therefore superior according to Gilbert, as it is a sign of a liberated being.

One of the elements of Epicurean teaching that philosophers have struggled with the most throughout history is the idea of abiding (katastemic) pleasure. It is often argued that lack of pain is not a definition of pleasure. This is a crucial aspect of the Epicurean art of living: our tradition teaches that a prudent person learns to be happy regardless of external factors and that it's possible and desirable to cultivate abiding pleasures via the philosophical disciplines.

Like Epicurus, Gilbert teaches that frequency is more important than intensity when it comes to positive experiences, and that small stuff (the simple pleasures) matters: these are things like a night out with friends, a movie with a loved one, the stuff fond memories are made of. His research also suggests that people tend to take more pleasure in experiences than in things, that is, relations make experiences fun and the ability to share a pleasant experience makes it much more memorable and enjoyable.

Hedonic Immunity

Gilbert says that synthetic happiness is artificial, but it's just as real as natural happiness and argues that, just as we have a physical immune system, we also seem to have a psychological immune system that helps us to cope with difficulties.

I should take a moment to elaborate the idea of hedonic immunity, which I believe has some merit within philosophical naturalism. Epicurean hedonism has been greatly misunderstood, in part, because of defamation by other philosophical schools and religions.

Epicurus did not teach so much that we should seek pleasure, but that we all do and that there are rational ways to do so. The pleasure principle helps all sentient beings to survive: by listening to the voice of Mother Nature, who speaks in the tone of suavity and of pleasure, sentient beings are driven to behavior that will ensure their survival. This is why eating and mating are pleasant, and it's why social entities whose safety is enhanced by the collective derive pleasure from grooming and friendship.

Epicurus encouraged us to trust anticipations or pre-existing ideas (along with sense data and the pleasure-pain mechanism) as part of the checks and balances used for our formulation of reality. Many of these anticipations are inherited instincts that helped our ancestors to survive. The infant's anticipation of the pleasures of lactation is an example of what feels like a collective memory of the species.

Throughout the history of life on earth, our ancestors going all the way back to the first forms of life progressively became better and more adapted at surviving in their environments. Only those who survived were able to successfully pass on their genes, so that our genetic makeup is the result of hundreds of millions of years of natural selection, of sentient beings who successfully listened to their ancestral biological wisdom and survival strategy.

Natural selection easily explains why pleasure is life's highest good, how pleasure as a goal is non-different from life as a goal, how our philosophy is a life-based naturalist philosophy, and why it makes sense to derive value and meaning from our inherent biological imperatives. Survival is made possible only if we listen to nature and pleasure is the suavity in the voice of nature which leads us to that which will help us thrive. By having an understanding of our biological anticipations and inherited instincts, we can properly understand why we all seek pleasure, as well as the probability raised by Dan Gilbert of hedonic immunity. We are built to recognize pleasure as the force that drives our evolution.

One final note on hedonic immunity, again drawing from biology: in recent years, a new field of gastro-neuroscience has emerged which studies the neurological system that humans have in their stomachs. The guts contain 100 million brain cells, which constitute a neural communication network the size of a cat's brain. The connection between moods and diet is now undeniable.

Michael Gershon (1999) calls the gut stomach our second brain. This gut brain manages not only digestion but also much of our immune system, as it is via the stomach that most germs and viruses enter our body.

If we do have a kind of psychological immune system, that may shed light on the psychosomatic symptoms of phenomena and diseases of the soul, which sometimes manifest as butterflies in the stomach, knots in our guts when we live through an emotional shock, or the visceral rage, anger or courage that we experience at times when we have an adrenaline rush.

I am reminded here of how, when philosopher Jean-Paul Sartre wrote a novel to dramatize existential angst, that he chose the title *Nausea*. This confirmed an intuitive insight that Epicurus also had about the relationship between the gut and the emotions, the instincts, and the soul. His other work *Being and Nothingness* seems to confirm that other fundamental concept in philosophical materialism: the fact that all reality is made up of the binary language of atoms and the void, another term for being and nothingness.

But I digress. It is known that many emotional and psychological problems are non-different from digestive symptoms: diabetes, depression, bulimia and anorexia are examples of dysfunctions that can be both psychological and digestive in nature and oftentimes have to do with an inaccurate appraisal of reality. The bulimic patient may only weigh 80 pounds, but still think she is obese and experience deep self-loathing. This may be an extreme example, but it's a revealing one.

If we take as premises that survival depends both on consumption and on being able to identify and find accurate pleasure in that which is good, then eating disorders represent an unwillingness or even an inability to survive. They are diseases of the soul. Future research on emotional wellbeing as it relates to the stomach, its brain and its functions, should further clarify the relationship between diet and our existential health.

Epicurus taught that our mortal souls are atomic, in other words, that the nervous system and the brain, with all its neural networks, together form the physical soul. Therefore, it is not difficult to surmise that our souls, in their natural and healthy state, know how to survive just as our bodies have the wisdom to survive and that they both have immune systems which are discernible in the body.

The stomach, being the seat of consumption, is therefore the seat of survival and should be targeted for future research around psychological health and hedonic immunity.

Hedonic Adaptation

It is at this point that we must tackle the principle of hedonic adaptation, also known as the hedonic treadmill. According to happiness researchers, the human mind has a more or less stable or habitual level of happiness that it returns to after the excitement of a good event or the disappointment of a difficulty.

Gilbert argues the case for synthetic happiness by citing the example of a lottery winner and a paraplegic who were both equally happy one year after, respectively, winning the lottery and losing both legs (Brickman et al., 1978). People seem to have a natural happiness baseline that they almost always return to after a sad or exciting experience.

If we do not understand and accept the temporary nature of pleasures, we fall under their spell, ever expecting more gratification, and we experience perturbance and perpetual disappointment. Constantly running after the objects of our desire, we are incomplete, not whole.

Research suggests that our brains probably behave in the same manner when we are addicted to hard drugs, to alcohol, to sugar (Hoebel et al., 2008), and to lovers (Thrasybule, 2012). The brain acts like it's addicted when we fall in love. When we are enslaved to our desires, our pleasure easily turns to pain. We unwisely go from satiation to craving.

Epicurus recognized the existence of hedonic adaptation and suggested the development of a regimen of varied, simple pleasures that generate no pain as a side effect, as well as a focus on development of our character and on mental pleasures, rather than relying on externals.

External factors have the power to affect happiness only temporarily whereas our attitudes toward external factors affect our set point of happiness. If we adjust our attitude in life, we live a more pleasant life and become more pleasant people. And so the wise Epicurean learns to develop a spiritual practice that focuses on cultivating the ability to experience abiding pleasure, the ability to synthesize happiness.

Abiding (katastemic) pleasure has been distinguished as the pleasure of being, whereas the pleasure of doing is dynamic (kinetic). Inert pleasure happens after our desires are sated, but it can also happen before a desire arises if we are mindful. In fact, practitioners of Zen meditation train their minds to cultivate a state of abiding peace and happiness by just being there, by just breathing with attention and calm. Breathing fresh air is the most basic of simple pleasures.

If the mind frequently wanders, one easy way to dismiss distractions and ensure that it remains focused is to concentrate on one's breath, and return to it, and return to it again and just be mindful of the present moment and the immediacy and details of the experience of just being. This is the basis of Zen practice, and ancient Epicureans were believed to engage in similar ascetic practices in order to keep their minds focused on the present moment.

It's unfortunate that so few of the 300 scrolls written by Epicurus survived. It's possible that many of his detailed explanations of abiding pleasure were in the sources that were destroyed, and then our job as philosophers seeking to revive Epicurean tradition is to fill in the blanks by cultivating a new asceticism, and then developing a comprehensive, modern theory and praxis of the pleasant life based on his insights and those of modern research.

Oftentimes it is said that abiding pleasure is merely the absence of pain, but by paying attention to that which is absent we are isolated from reality as it is. In the absence of pain, where does our attention go? Ponder that desire is the state of lacking and wanting something that is not there, whereas pleasure is the state of relishing what is there. Ergo, a pleasant life can only be lived if we train our minds daily to relish and enjoy whatever is there, however prosaic it may seem. An Epicurean at every moment must discover the pleasure of breathing, the pleasure of walking, of eating a simple fruit, the pleasure of a friend's association, rather than mindlessly going through these motions.

Let us live while we are alive. —Epicurus

When I experimented with vegetarianism, I learned that Hindu tradition calls for there being food in every color on the plate: some red lentils, a little green spinach, white rice, and so on. This is to ensure that our diet meets all of our nutritional needs.

Hedonic adaptation, and the fact that we easily and frequently get tired of new and old pleasures, leads us to the importance of variety in our pleasure regimen. Just as we need variety in our diet in order to meet our physical needs, so do we need variety in our pleasant activities in order to live a good life. We should therefore develop a regimen of various pleasures to fill our day, some productive and others purely for leisure.

Now, the most practical way to do this, other than to ensure that we do the work that we love and that we love the work that we do in order to make a living, is to pay attention to how we satisfy our most basic needs, those desires that are necessary and therefore whose fulfillment we cannot escape, like food, safety, and association. I will discuss friendship, autarchy, and diet in future chapters.

More Good News About the Good Life: Bad Things are Easy to Endure

The fourth remedy in Epicurus' Tetrapharmakon is a reminder that sources of physical pain and mental anguish exist, but that these are easy to endure. We will confront difficulties in life: anyone who denies this is seeking false hopes and will be disappointed. People will die. We will get sick and suffer injury. We will have difficult relationships at work or in our social and family lives. We will lose friends. It's unwise to be unprepared for unexpected change when life is constantly in flux and the only permanent thing is change. Many wisdom traditions, most notably among them Hinduism and Buddhism, derive consolation from the transient nature of all sense perception and experience.

O son of Kunti, the nonpermanent appearance of happiness
and distress, and their disappearance in due course, are like
the appearance and disappearance of winter and summer
seasons. They arise from sense perception, O scion of Bharata,
and one must learn to tolerate them without being disturbed.
—Bhagavad Gita 2:14

We can draw strength and insight from the impermanent nature of reality. While it is true that the pleasure of association with others is temporary, it's also true that when people die or leave us, we mourn them at first, but we soon recover and fill the gap with new interests. The pain of loss is temporary. When we fall ill, our immune systems immediately begin to fight the disease and we soon recover and forget that we were ever sick. It's unfair to think of illness as being greater than it really is, when we've spent most of our lives in good health and it's unlikely that a week-long flu or an ear infection will remain forever, painful as they may be.

Even with chronic disease, we eventually get used to it and are able to find pleasure in other things in the midst of our discomfort. We construct our experience of reality at every moment. The ability to quickly dismiss pain and focus on a source of joy is exhibited by children, who often fall while they're playing and hit their heads or knees, cry for about a minute, then get up, start playing again, and in a matter of seconds they're laughing hysterically. Where did the pain go? Well, it was there, but now it doesn't matter. The pleasant, wholesome state of not knowing physical pain is known as *aponia*.

Most of us have forgotten this basic innocence of being a fresh person and choosing a fresh reality at every second, but this ability can be cultivated. Also, when physical pain is severe, we may encourage the brain's release of endorphins via exercise or dietary means: hot peppers, for instance, aid with pain tolerance (Yao, 2009). Means of releasing endorphins will be discussed in detail in the chapter on developing a hedonic regime.

In the case of mental anxiety, cognitive therapy can be applied to it. The insight of impermanence still holds true: if we are anxious about loss of a job, we should consider that after a period of unemployment there will come a period of employment, and that when we view time from the perspective of the long term we tend to see loss as a boon. We would not have been able to find the better paying job, meet the more affable supervisor or the current romantic partner, if we had not lost the previous job or relationship.

Just as we allow ourselves to get lost in the worries of the moment and experience anxiety, we can also forget this moment and attempt to see it from a distance in order to dismiss anxiety. What advice would you today give the person that you were five or ten years ago, when you went through a terrible moment in life? Do your temporary troubles not seem much less insurmountable now than they did then? It's healthy, from time to time, to gain insight from the long-term perspective. I am reminded of the *It Gets Better Project*, where older members of the LGBT community and allies share testimonies for gay and lesbian youth, who make up between 20-40 percent of homeless youth in America and frequently have to deal with rejection, bullying, emotional abuse and violence (Ray, 2006).

Also, ponder that by being mindful of painful phenomena, we can learn to understand the sources of our pain, cultivate patience and compassion for self and others, become stronger in the face of suffering, and we gain many other insights. Being attentively mindful of the phenomena of attachment, impermanence, suffering and death is considered a valued form of contemplation in Buddhism. In our tradition, we speak of living the examined life, but the process and the use of the practice is similar. A serene cultivation of the attention produces a fortification around one's mind.

Therefore, anyone who wishes to live a pleasant life must train his or her attention in order to cope heroically and mindfully with physical pain and mental anxiety.

New Verbiage

Abiding (or Katastemic) Pleasure
Aponia
Dynamic (or Kinetic) Pleasure
The Pleasure Regimen
Remedy
Tetrapharmakon

Task: The Task List

During this chapter I mentioned Harvard research that concludes that the wandering mind is unhappiest whereas the mind that is focused and rapt on only one activity, whether it be categorized as productivity or leisure, is happiest. The remedy, then, becomes focus and concentration on one task at a time. If we try to juggle too many balls at one time, we lose them.

Be present in the present. Train yourself to fully focus on the moment you are living and the task you are completing. If you are working, work. If you are reading, just read mindfully. If you are dancing, dance. If you are singing, just sing. Immerse yourself fully in the book, the film, the association of your good friend, or whatever you're doing; relish the plate that you're eating regardless of how simple it may be. Rediscover how to relish the sweetness of fruits, the natural high of exercise, the mellows of your favorite song.

A life of hedonism must not be an unproductive one. It's important to have an agenda, a calendar, and a daily task list. It's one of the habits of efficient people. It ensures that we don't designate too much time to vain pursuits. But another side effect of having a task list, particularly for busy times or busy people, is that it diminishes the anxiety of having too many things on our minds and allows us to more easily focus on the task at hand. With this tool, we are able to focus on doing the house chores, then focus on reading, then focus on exercise, then focus on working from home, etc. without being overwhelmed by the many things we must do.

Resolve to always have a task list, particularly if your mind tends to wander. It's never been easier to carry a task list around. Cellphones and other such modern gadgets can be used as tools to increase productivity and focus. Most of them have built-in calendar and alarm apps where we can give ourselves reminders or write notes to ourselves.

Task: Introspecting On Fears, Needs and Desires

Use your journal to name your needs, desires and fears, and begin to develop a regimen of simple, easy to attain pleasures based on the insights attained. Periodically, you may want to indulge in an unnecessary pleasure. Enjoy this! But also enjoy the simple day-to-day ones!

If you are religious, evaluate whether you have lingering fear-based beliefs and how you may educate yourself about the true nature of things in order to overcome them.

Begin to gather and nurture your own wisdom tradition as a philosopher. What other remedies or methods have you learned that have helped you to cope with difficulties, cultivate virtues, or better yourself? What are some of the prudent and important things that your ancestors and mentors taught you?

Attend to your necessary pleasures (those that generate pain when unfulfilled) as your first priority, then you can easily dismiss the unnecessary and vain ones. Notice especially the desires that generate pain when fulfilled versus those that don't: if the meal that you were craving gives you acidity or pain in your stomach, it's clearly unintelligent to continue yielding to it. One remedy to help dismiss unnecessary desires is to choose a word that makes them easy to dismiss, like 'silly' or 'taboo,' then immediately when you're visited by that desire, use the word and shift your attention to something else.

Task: Daily Regimen of Abiding and Dynamic Pleasures

Once you have articulated your resolution to cultivate a happy mind and character by using applied philosophy, you should keep a gratitude journal. Take time daily to be thankful and appreciative for family, for friends, for those you love (whether they're here now or were here in the past), for the land you live in, for the supply or abundance of your basic needs, for the food you eat, for the colors and beauty in your world and the things you're learning every day. In this day and age, this is easy to do on a smartphone or tablet.

As for active pleasures, consider taking up a sport, a hobby, or learning meditative practices. Exercise may sound like work but it's actually an amazing mood booster and the euphoria of the runner's high is a natural anesthetic that helps the brain ignore pain (University of Bonn, 2008).

References:

Avena, Nicole et al. "Evidence for sugar addiction: Behavioral and neurochemical effects of intermittent, excessive sugar intake." (National Institutes of Health, 2008). Retrieved from http://www.ncbi.nlm.nih.gov/pmc/articles/PMC2235907/

Brickman, P. et al. "Lottery winners and accident victims: is happiness relative?" *PubMed* (August, 1978). Retrieved from http://www.ncbi.nlm.nih.gov/pubmed/690806

Gershon, Michael M.D. *The Second Brain: A Groundbreaking New Understanding of Nervous Disorders of the Stomach and Intestine.* (New York: Harper Perennial, 1999).

Gilbert, Daniel. *Stumbling on Happiness.* (New York: Random House, 2007).

Kahneman, Daniel and Deaton, Angus. "High income improves evaluation of life but not emotional well-being." (Princeton University, 2010). Retrieved from http://www.princeton.edu/~deaton/downloads/deaton_kahneman_high_income_improves_evaluation_August2010.pdf

Paul, Gregory. "Cross-National Correlations of Quantifiable Societal Health with Popular Religiosity and Secularism in the Prosperous Democracies." *Journal of Religion & Society,* Volume 7 (2005). Retrieved from http://moses.creighton.edu/jrs/2005/2005-11.pdf

Ray, N. "Lesbian, gay, bisexual and transgender youth: An epidemic of homelessness." (New York: National Gay and Lesbian Task Force Policy Institute and the National Coalition for the Homeless, 2006).

Thomas, Stanley J. & Danko, William D. *The Millionaire Next Door: The Surprising Secrets of America's Wealthy.* (Lanham, MD: Taylor Trade Publishing, 2010).

Thrasybule, Linda. "Falling In Love Affects Brain Much Like Addiction, Scientists Say." *Huffington Post,* February 13, 2012. Retrieved from http://www.huffingtonpost.com/2012/02/13/falling-in-love-triggers-brain-changes_n_1273196.html

University of Bonn. "Runners' High Demonstrated: Brain Imaging Shows Release Of Endorphins In Brain." *ScienceDaily,* March 6, 2008. Retrieved from http://www.sciencedaily.com/releases/2008/03/080303101110.htm

Yao, Jing and Qin, Feng. "Interaction with phosphoinositides confers adaptation onto the TRPV1pain receptor." *PLOS Biology,* February 24, 2009. http://www.plosbiology.org/article/info%3Adoi%2F10.1371%2Fjournal.pbio.1000046

V

EPICUREAN THERAPY

Vain is the word of a philosopher which does not heal any suffering of humankind. For just as there is no profit in medicine if it does not expel the diseases of the body, so there is no profit in philosophy either, if it does not expel the suffering of the mind.

—Epicurus

As we've seen, the redeeming goal of Epicureanism is to become a tool kit for our flourishing, for dealing with our difficulties and for cultivating a mind and a life that leads to happiness—a goal similar to that of The Happiness Project on today's internet. It is meant to be an ongoing therapeutic practice of self-betterment and an ethical lifestyle in the truest sense of the word: the aim is not only to live a pleasant life, but also to participate in the creation of a sub-culture, or perhaps a counter-culture, that is conducive to a pleasant life for all of our philosopher friends.

Ancient Epicureans believed that this therapeutic process had to be ongoing because of the corruption of society. This is still the case. We live in a consumerist society where vain and empty desires and values are constantly praised and celebrated in mass media. Epicurus advised his followers to be in frequent association with people of like mind, as this is essential both for living a pleasant life and for developing good habits.

The Garden did not give diplomas or graduate people once they attained a certain level of insight: it functioned, instead, as a community of friends who created a pleasant environment for living the analyzed life, engaged in philosophical discourse, and explored their adventure of self-betterment and Epicurean therapy together. This community was meant to encourage the disarming and abandoning of vices, or bad habits, and the development and cultivation of virtues, or good habits that produce a pleasant character.

On Frank Speech and Suavity

Epicurus was critical of the sophistry of other philosophical schools: that ability to twist meanings and words, and to convince others even of untruths. There are times when philosophers use rhetoric to conceal truth. Aristotle considered rhetoric to be part of the *organon*, the toolkit of the philosopher. But the Epicurean *organon* employed instead suavity: the art of kind, sweet speech that Epicurean friends were known for in antiquity.

True philosophy, Epicurus believed, is not about verbal ability. Epicureans hold truth in high regard and always prefer the plain, concise, clear truth over dishonest wordplay, employing *parrhesia*, which translates as frank speech, in their interactions with each other.

But sometimes the truth can be difficult to swallow and, if not careful, we can easily seem cynical when acting in service of truth. We must be mindful of the content of our character and the true purpose behind our words when we engage others in philosophical discourse, and even in trivial conversation.

> *Always tell the truth with kindness. Never lie with kindness, or tell the truth with bitterness.*
> —Sai Baba

By always telling the truth with kindness, we encourage people around us to always be authentic, at ease in their own skin, mindful, and insightful. And so the art of suavity, the art of kindly telling the truth, the art of wholesome communication, is a necessary Epicurean virtue.

There are many ways of saying things. When we truly care about others, we should seek to give them insights that will help them to better themselves and to suffer less. Epicurus considered those who don't tell us the truth to be false friends: untruth is a sign of unfaithfulness. A vaccine may be painful, but it's necessary at times: so with words of truth.

Ancient Epicureans had a system of mutual criticism, which evolved into a central aspect of the tradition. This system of mutual criticism is discussed at length by Norman W. Dewitt in his piece titled *Organization and Procedure in Epicurean Groups,* where he explained how crucial it is to Epicureanism as a practice, how it requires trust, and how one must learn to be humble and accept corrections.

The Therapy of Desire (Nussbaum, 1996) mentions the asymmetry of roles between the teacher/philosopher and the pupil/patient. The Epicurean student must have the trust and initiative to approach the Guide, and the Guide must be knowledgeable and apply the right amount of harshness or suavity.

And so the dynamic that emerges within the Gardens is one where those that are more knowledgeable are expected to serve as mentors to newer Epicureans. According to DeWitt, these Guides are also expected to abide by a set of rules, to never abuse their status, to employ suavity in their mentoring process, and they in turn have to answer to more senior Epicureans so that there are checks and balances.

Suavity seems to have been the social lubricant in this process. One of the tasks of every Epicurean is to cultivate suavity, to learn the ability to prudently tell the truth with kindness.

The Garden as a Refuge

The Epicurean process of self-betterment may sometimes require times of retreat, re-focus and separation from other views. To cite the frequently used metaphor of medicine which is prevalent in all the therapeutic Hellenistic philosophies, we may think of the Garden as a place where we can rehabilitate ourselves after an accident or illness in order to make full recovery, except that here we are treating the diseases of the soul. Likewise, if the disease is chronic, it may require more frequent visits.

Because the process of mutual correction needs trust and the willingness to be criticized and to become vulnerable with other friends, it requires a safe space that must be set aside and consecrated especially for this process where people feel comfortable being themselves. This space can be symbolic (a circle of friends) or physical (the Garden).

Also, if it is true that our groundless opinions are based on societal expectations and that culture has a corrupting influence on the soul, then we need a subversive counter-culture of virtue. The Garden, as a spiritual metaphor, serves this role.

Diagnosis

Perhaps the most crucial part of Epicurean therapy has to do with the process of accurately identifying the moral enemies: habits that are symptomatic of, and leading to, unhappiness, or those that impede our flourishing. Metaphors from the field of medicine abound in Epicurean tradition. Without an accurate diagnosis, it is impossible to seek remedies. The process by which moral disease is identified involves various means, including confession and informing.

Epicurean confession probably inspired the Catholic sacrament meant to purge guilt from the soul. However, this confession is not based on a punitive cosmovision. The idea is not to punish but to diagnose and treat diseases of the soul. It was Philodemus who said we must accuse ourselves before our Epicurean Guides if we err. This is the best way to begin the process of addressing our symptoms, so that they may be identified for diagnosis and treatment. By doing this we also earn the trust and goodwill of the Epicurean Guide.

An alternative way of identifying symptoms of moral disease was by informing, where pupils confess to the Guide on behalf of each other.

For an Epicurean who lacks a therapeutic community and wishes to engage in the process of self-betterment, it is necessary to begin to work on the task of cultivating potential philosopher friends who are familiar with Epicurean practice. Friends are useful because they can give less subjective, more balanced feedback. Also, an independent Epicurean should employ frank speech via journaling and writing about his progress. In this way, the philosopher develops a habit of daily self-examination.

In all cases, the process is the same: we bring the moral flaws into the open and we name the inner enemy. If we do not name the moral enemy and learn to relate to the enemy as such, we become lax and allow our bad habits to steer the boat. An Autarch must not allow mutiny in her own soul. Once we've named the enemy, we can then assign ourselves remedies, tasks to purge the enemy from our character.

For instance, there may be a type of person that we dislike and, upon every encounter, we become angry. Or it may be an individual, someone we have to see daily at work or school, or in our circle of friends. We may gain the insight that many people have bad habits or qualities that we dislike mixed in with good ones that we find common ground with. If we have to encounter a disliked person daily, we may realize that it's not worth it to let the negative feelings perturb us that frequently.

It's usually a matter of breaking the ice. It is key that we learn to laugh at ourselves when we're uptight. Sometimes it takes only one smile, one joke, or one shared happy moment to turn ill will into goodwill; or it may take friendly small-talk to release tension between two people. There are many simple remedies and experiments that we can try out, based on the situation, to begin finding common ground with those whom we dislike.

It is impossible and impractical to be everyone's friend: if friendship is impossible, then Epicurus advises that we keep the distance in the service of ataraxia.

Treatment by Argument

*We cast off common customs just as we would do to wicked
men who have been causing great harm for a long time.*

—Vatican Sayings 46

One of the underlying premises of Epicurean therapy is
that emotions, desires and appetites—however irrational they
may seem—have a cognitive, as well as an unconscious, component. Furthermore, it is understood that there are false and
true beliefs that feed our emotions and appetites.

In other words, whenever we have desires that are not natural and necessary, these are the result of wrong views that we
have acquired from culture or from bad association and we
can engage these desires in argument in order to deflate and
easily discard them.

If we find ourselves wanting to drive a Porsche or wanting to live in an overpriced house in a certain neighborhood,
and we find ourselves ready to get into considerable debts in
order to attain these things, it may be possible to save ourselves from needless sacrifice to pay for these things by considering the true reasons for having them. Perhaps we have
unanalyzed feelings of envy towards a friend or a desire to
impress co-workers that we did not previously acknowledge.
Perhaps we got hypnotized by a commercial and never really
stopped to analyze it, or our neighbors are the ones who wish
to have these things and we have attained their views without putting thought into whether or not things make people
happy, and whether we can be perfectly happy without them.
Or maybe it's the pride of family members or even the good
wishes of well-meaning strangers that we're trying to satisfy,
and not our own.

Therefore, we utilize arguments that describe and evaluate
empty, harmful beliefs that cause pain and sustain our vain
and empty emotions and appetites in order to weaken them.
These arguments can incorporate reminders of how we get

tired of new things once we get used to them. We can then easily reject improper and needless desires that have been proven to be based on wrong views and assign a process for correcting these habits.

It is useful to allow the voice of the inner enemy to participate in our arguments. There are sometimes important insights that can be derived from the process of naming the enemy and arguing with it and which, if addressed, can help to avoid different kinds of perturbances in the future.

Epicurus taught that our bad habits and emotions generally are caused by dispositions or tendencies that lead to anger, fear, lust, addictions, etc. It is as important to detect and name these dispositions as it is to detect and name the actual vice, its evident symptom. Arguments help to uncover the underlying intrapsychic drama that leads to the bad habit.

For an individual Epicurean who lacks a Guide, one way to argue against the habit is by imagining a conversation between the philosopher and his habit, which is personified and given a name and an identity, maybe even a history of its own. This can be done through journaling.

Did your habit arise after you ended a bad relation? Or when you started associating with a certain person? Maybe you can treat the habit as a contagious virus that you acquired from a friend with whom you failed to set healthy boundaries. Much of our speech, consumption, false beliefs and other habits are acquired through unwholesome association.

For instance, it may be that we are in the habit of spending vast amounts of money on ice cream, cigars, coffee, or some other food or habit of consumption that is overpriced and lacks nutritional value. For the sake of an example, if we subject our habits of consumerism to this therapy, we may uncover an anxiety that arises from the habit of wanting to have or do rather than a habit of being satisfied, abiding in tranquility.

But we may also find our bad habits arguing that we work too hard and have little time for fun and leisure, or that we are always giving in our relationships and no one ever gives to us, etc. We should begin by recognizing and owning these feelings, grateful for their insights. We can then decide whether to fully give up a bad habit, or to diminish the influence of this desire and limit our indulgence in it to once a week, rather than two or three times per week. It is sometimes not a bad thing to indulge in certain desires once in a blue moon, but it often becomes prudent to challenge the desire if it becomes a habit or addiction.

Our past decisions and hardened beliefs sometimes think they're doing something for us, protecting us. But sometimes these unconscious devices misfire. For instance, a young woman who was abandoned by her father at a young age may decide that men are never to be trusted, and may never allow herself to be able to properly bond with men as an adult, even if she meets the most caring gentleman, the man of her dreams.

She will be unable to confront and transform the belief that all men are never to be trusted, unless and until she names her past decision as an inner enemy and argues with it, probably for an extended period of time until a new conviction becomes powerful in her soul.

Another scheme that oftentimes becomes counter-productive has to do with old enemies. Harboring grudges is very harmful for one's stable well-being and happiness, rarely harms the target of our hatred and is unproductive. It may be that the old enemy no longer matters, has moved on to other interests, or has learned her lesson and changed her heart. If the enemy is within and not without, then it is within that we must confront it before conflict spills into the outer world.

Because the process of argument is meant to be purgative, used to remove moral flaws, this process can be harsh. Sometimes it's hard for reason to persuade emotion or desire, and a more confrontational approach is needed. The Guide can sweeten this bitterness when he concocts a remedy for our moral disease by praise and encouragement when we do good things.

Preventive Therapy: Reasonings

In our tradition, reasonings are sober discussions evaluating Epicurean doctrine on its own right, or as it applies to our lives. I use the word sober to differentiate our philosophical tradition of reasonings from the Rastafarian tradition by the same name, which consists of sacramental smoking of ganjah and discussion of Bible-based theology. In philosophy, the use of mind-altering substances is highly controversial and discouraged. True reasonings require sobriety.

Through this process we may, for instance, evaluate and separate the healthy and natural desires from the empty and unnatural ones. We can then observe the ways in which natural desires are easy to satisfy, and the ways in which unnatural desires are based on groundless opinion. This strengthens our conviction and gives us more lucidity in our understanding of the Epicurean theory of human happiness.

By doing this, we may become aware of how easy it is to satisfy our natural desire for food with a small amount of rice or bread, versus how difficult or expensive it is to satisfy the need for specific foods that we sometimes crave, or versus effects of overeating on our health. If we engage in reasonings, we can assimilate insights without having to make costly mistakes.

One of the products of reasonings is an increased certainty and faith in Epicurus and his teaching. Epicureanism treats faith as a virtue. However this Epicurean faith is understood not as our culture's corrupt conception of faith as blind belief in things that cannot be proven but, in its original context, as trust. Once we have identified a trustworthy friend, a well-wisher who truly wants us to flourish and who supports our process of self-betterment and who is knowledgeable about reality and the science of happiness, then it becomes a virtue to place our faith in that person or teaching.

A strong faith and conviction serves as a remedy against existential anxieties about the afterlife and about future pains or pleasures. Conviction and certainty of Epicurean teachings also helps to strengthen confidence in our ability to steer the helm of our own destiny by choosing which desires to dismiss and which ones to limit or pursue at each moment.

> *When nine hundred years old you reach, look*
> *as good, you will not.*
>
> —Yoda

We may think of reasonings as a type of vaccine or preventive remedy. For instance, if we subject our desire for immortality to reasonings, we can expose how empty it is, perhaps the vainest of desires.

We may, firstly, consider Lucretius' argument from his poem *On the Nature of Things*, that old people must die in order to allow for new people to populate the world, and we may ponder the pain of surviving everyone we ever loved. Death, our final tax payment to the rest of nature, may even be seen as much needed rest after a long battle with chronic disease.

We may also consider how one gets tired of pleasures after they no longer seem new, or perhaps how much more difficult it would be to experience pleasure at 900 years of age than it is as a young person. Also, we are much more at ease when we accept our natural limitations.

If anything, we can choose to turn our empty desire for immortality into an insight and interpret it as an affirmation of abiding pleasure and of the value that we find in the mere fact that we exist.

There are times when fear or anticipation of future pain, as well as apprehension about future availability of a pleasure, can become a source of anxiety. We torture ourselves with anxieties about future acquisition of wealth. If we've been betrayed before, we may worry excessively about the future loyalties of loved ones. Of all the gods, Fortune (in her many expressions and personifications) has always been among the most feared.

If we find out that we have an illness, it would be unfair to abuse ourselves emotionally by playing out future scenarios of physical suffering or death. It is unfair to expect that, after many years of normal health, we will succumb to persistent years of agony merely because we encountered an instance of poor health. Philodemus spoke about how we should nurture hope that we will be healthy and recover from disease, as we usually do. Through applying therapeutic reasoning frequently, we maintain good philosophical hygiene and prevent anxieties and bitterness from taking root in the soul.

Repetition and Memorization

Many diseases of the soul are tied to ignorance in the form of the false beliefs underlying them, which were often treated through the affirmation and memorization of the right beliefs contained in the teaching. Epicurus taught that, through repetition, these right beliefs become powerful in the soul. This practice was so widespread that memory handbooks, or *epitomai*, were frequently used both for repetition and as learning manuals.

It was expected that through repetition and memorization the teaching would strengthen its roots and become powerful. In neurological terms, we can understand today that new neural pathways are cultivated through this exercise. Recent studies are confirming that meditation, including focused mantra recitation, changes the brain faster and more dramatically than previously thought. This new, promising field of research is known as neuroplasticity.

According to *Women's Fitness* magazine, neuroscientist Marian Diamond, from the University of California, found chanting helps block the release of stress hormones and increases immune function, while another neuroscientist, Dr. Alan Watkins at Imperial College London, showed that while chanting your heart rate and blood pressure will drop to its lowest of the day. (Boggenpoel, 2013).

Whether it's praying the rosary, or chanting the Hare Krishna mantra, the benefits are the same. While this does not confirm the supernatural beliefs of the Catholics, Buddhists or Hare Krishnas, it does grant scientific merit to the practice of chanting and reciting mantras. Many modern musicians, such as Krishna Das, Jai Uttal, and even Boy George and the former Beatle George Harrison have taken up the yoga practice of blissful chanting and incorporated them into their art.

Enhancements to meditation and repetition can be added to produce a much more pleasant relaxation ritual. Research by Johns Hopkins University and the Hebrew University reveals that incense has anti-depressant and psycho-active properties (Moussaieff et al., 2008). The use of incense in meditation creates a pleasant atmosphere and alleviates anxiety. I've always been fond of lavender, sandalwood, cedar, and other aromas and noticed their mood enhancing effects, but now there's science behind incense burning and more reasons than ever to adopt the practice.

But there are more reasons to add incense to our practice: our sense of smell processes data in the brain's limbic system, which is sometimes called the emotional brain and ties to our memory banks. A familiar smell can easily evoke memories and emotions tied to our familiarity with people, places, experiences, and foods that make us feel safe and comfortable.

Memorization of Epicurean doctrines was particularly useful in the treatment of fear of death and irrational fear of the gods: a strong commitment to naturalist philosophical conviction can help build a strong fortification around the mortal soul.

In the brief time I've spent promoting Epicureanism as a contemporary alternative, I've encountered several survivors of Christian cults, some of whom were severely damaged by their upbringing in fear-based belief and must spend years reprogramming their minds. We have no reason to suppose that there weren't people similarly damaged in pagan antiquity, particularly when we consider that child sacrifice and human sacrifice were practiced routinely in the world of Epicurus' time. Because of the traumatic nature of these experiences, an intensified temporary regimen of repetition and memorization might be one of the most useful remedies to try out in these cases in order to fully purge the soul of the vestiges of these experiences.

Assigning Other Remedies

We must at all times be pragmatic. Many of the ills of the soul require multiple remedies, not just one. If the enemy of endless chatter keeps us from sleeping or focusing on the things we're doing, perhaps once we name this enemy, we can start having five minutes of recharging our batteries through silence before proceeding with the day, in addition to abandoning the use of coffee and adopting caffeine-free tea instead and working through some of our other habits that may add to our agitation.

One remedy used in ancient therapy consisted of re-labeling people or things that we are attached to in order to reveal the empty nature of the desire. Perhaps the person responsible for arousing intense, frustrated sexual passion can be re-labeled in such a way that makes him or her easy to dismiss. If another person arouses intense hatred or anger, perhaps we can get accustomed to avoiding a direct reference and using an indirect one that does not evoke strong emotional responses.

We do not have to ignore people who annoy us. Sometimes that misfires and those same people become elephants in the room. They gain power when ignored. Aversion is a form of attachment. The idea is to create a label that represents an objective, detached identity: it is just what it is, nothing more. There is no intense emotional response: no detachment, no attachment.

As for other remedies, there is in the new thought movement a modern tradition of using affirmations. They consist of repeating good qualities, outcomes or attributes to ourselves as if they were real, things like "Life is good," "People are kind to me today," "I naturally attract wealth," etc. Can they work in Epicurean therapy?

One of the premises behind the practice of repetition is that it is meant to affirm, to make firm, the right views and to replace false beliefs. Although many affirmations sound like mere wishful thinking, Epicurus did teach that nature makes it easy to procure the things that make life worth living and easy to dismiss the things that are unnecessary for true happiness. As long as these practices do not contradict a naturalist understanding of reality or give false hopes or false promises (immortality, etc.), then there is no reason not to use them.

Dealing with Anger

Philosophy would be castrating if it didn't allow us to experience what the philosophers of old knew as natural anger. In her article *The Necessity of Anger in Philodemus' On Anger*, Elizabeth Asmis argues the case that the same categories that exist for desires in Epicureanism can be applied to anger. Arguing based on Philodemus' writings, she says that anger can be natural and necessary, it can be natural and unnecessary or unnatural and unnecessary—and therefore empty and, furthermore, useless.

Anger becomes necessary, even for a wise person, when there is an alienating assumption of voluntary harm that may take away life, bodily health, or happiness. This assumption must not be based on false beliefs. For instance, we may not personify fate and curse Fortuna, God or an evil spirit for our bad luck and call our rage natural and necessary. Philodemus also categorized anger that merely hates or places blame as foolish. But if a thug threatens the life of our loved ones, or if a sexual partner turns physically abusive, then anger is a moral necessity.

Ancient Epicureans taught that anger, in its fetal stage, originates as a preliminary bite or pang, an impression of injury. Our sense of indignation evolves into natural, rational anger if judged properly and endorsed. If allowed to run out of control, then it breeds brutality and savagery and becomes irrational.

Rational, necessary anger is moderate, calculated, and almost never takes the form of madness or rage (this would be based on the calculated benefits of said rage). It is here that hedonic calculus must be addressed, as the notions of rational anger and useless anger are best explained in light of it.

A rational person makes a comparative measurement of losses due to anger so that, in the end, anger must result in net gain to himself, otherwise it's empty. Rational anger is not punitive, but seeks to remove pain and restore the pleasant life. Therefore, punishment shouldn't be excessive, continuous or without a cause. Philodemus taught that natural, rational anger measures hedonic calculus: it calculates the expected pain and pleasure and seeks a net gain. This process is, of course, to a great extent subjective but it's the most—perhaps the only-- scientific approach we have to the moral question of anger.

For the sake of an example, road rage generates natural and (most people would argue) necessary anger. If someone cuts us off while we're driving, or ignores street signs and nearly causes an accident, we may calculate that we can easily continue driving and that it's not worth the five or ten minutes of justifiable anger. If we see that the person driving is being reckless or seems under the influence of alcohol and might put a life at risk, then the guilt we would feel if we don't act would weigh heavily on our decision to call the authorities. To speak concretely: we must calculate whether the pain of being angry outweighs the pleasure of not feeling guilty if an accident happened, which could have been avoided.

Natural and necessary anger is easily awakened when our natural and necessary desires are frustrated. Let's consider, for instance, shelter or food. If Hermarchus has a roommate who frequently takes and loses his keys and locks him out of the apartment, or who eats the last bit of food available in the kitchen knowing that Hermarchus won't get paid for another five days, then Hermarchus' anger would be natural and rational.

Any punitive action taken against his roommate would have to include a calculation of pain versus pleasure that would derive from it and its goal would be to prevent future harm. Clearly, the issues have to be addressed. If a tense conversation seems to fix the problems in their household, there may be little need to proceed with punishment for now. It may be that, knowing his roommate or considering the frequency of the negligence, Hermarchus chooses never to trust him again with the keys, chooses to store his food in a place that is not accessible, or perhaps even decides that they can't be roommates and someone must find a new apartment. Hermarchus must, in whatever he decides, measure his risks and the potential to remove pain.

Philodemus argued that slander, bad treatment, or abuse must arouse anger. There would be no justice in society, and it would degenerate into hellish existence, if there was no righteous, justified anger. Drawing from imagery and metaphors in nature, we may think of anger as a violent, yet creative force. Just as volcanoes erupt and produce new islands which later go on to become places where life can thrive and renew itself, in the same way rational, natural anger can become a force for social justice and positive change. Although it is unpleasant, if hedonic calculus is properly carried out, it leads to pleasure just as pain can and does lead to pleasure in many other instances (the pursuit of an educational goal which requires considerable sacrifices, a relationship that has ups and downs but over the long term produces a pleasant life, etc.).

On the other hand, unprofessional bosses and co-workers oftentimes create unwholesome work environments because of their uncontrolled rage. If a supervisor is a tyrant who gets habitually angered by small things, this anger —in addition to making him ugly and mad—is oftentimes useless, unnecessary and unnatural. If two workers chat casually during their shift, and if this does not generate a loss in revenue or productivity but the boss' anger is harmful to the morale of the workers, the uselessness and irrationality of this uncalculated anger is evident.

If an unnecessary and unnatural desire is frustrated, wasting time in anger is likewise considered empty and forbidden in Epicureanism. If we desired needless amounts of wealth or fame and our friend Hermarchus was busy at the Garden and forgot to purchase a lottery ticket or failed to drive us to the American Idol audition, it may be more intelligent to laugh at the situation than to be angry, particularly when little can be done to change it.

Our appraisal of anger, like the entirety of our therapy, should consider imperturbability as the ultimate goal: a life of serenity. Like all things in Epicureanism, rational anger should only be a tool, a remedy and a means to a pleasant life.

We should think of our souls as a tranquil lake. At times the winds create gentle, or even moderately agitated waves, but the lake always returns to its natural, clear and even state. So with our minds: they should remain lucid and our state of equanimity should be considered as normalcy. If we have not habituated our minds to easily become like a tranquil lake, then steps should be taken to achieve this goal.

On the Treatment of Anger

Chronic rage, like depression (which is a chronic sadness), is a disease of the soul characterized by particular symptoms. It's an anger that is obsessive about retaliation, persistent, out of control, intense and violent. It is not the natural, controlled, calculated, rational anger of the philosopher but something bestial and dehumanizing. We must first vilify the chronic disease of anger by diagnosing it, naming it and declaring it an enemy.

One treatment for this which was used by Philodemus and other philosophers in antiquity is known as seeing before the eyes. It consists of the Epicurean Guide confronting the patient with the consequences of chronic rage as a vivid depiction, a visualization where the repercussions and effects of anger in relations and in the ability to enjoy life every day are clearly presented as if they were present here and now. Insight into the future chain of events created by our mindless acts is a sign of prudence, which has among its definitions "the ability to think ahead."

This is done using rhetoric. It is a verbal exercise for the Guide and a visualization exercise for the patient. The practice requires the attribution of a vivid, horrific identity to anger, the inner enemy.

Presumably, a similar vilification of the moral disease may have been carried out for depression. If not, there is no reason why a depressed person should not try this, perhaps via journaling, and take note of the long-term results.

Physical signs of rage were used in ancient descriptions of symptoms by ancient philosophers, I suspect as a technique for vilification of the vice. We still speak in terms of the face reddening as blood rushes to the head when people get angry, of fuming, heavy breathing, screaming, becoming mad, and other behaviors that take place when people are possessed by rage. They're invariably related to heat, perhaps because of the effects of anger on our adrenaline, our heart rate, and our blood circulation.

Many cultures speak of irascible people as hot-headed. When I practiced zen meditation, I became very aware of where in my body the different kinds of anxiety and stress lodged themselves, and applied massages as well as the practice of tensing those muscles as I breathed in and loosening them as I breathed out. Many of my emotional apprehensions affected my gut area, which I loosened and treated with lower belly breathing techniques.

My forehead was always the recipient of mental stress, as well as the back part of the scalp. This stress had been constant and had taken its toll on me. I suspect that many or most students and people who engage in intellectual activities often deal with similar forms of stress. Although it's important to have a vibrant intellectual life, it's also important to get out of our heads from time to time and to engage in a variety of pleasant non-intellectual activities.

Epicurus teaches that the soul is atomic, that is, there is no boundary between body and soul. We are embodied beings. If the symptoms of the diseases of the soul are physical, then it makes sense that physical remedies must be applied also.

I've always admired how, in African culture and spirituality, there is no boundary between the soul and the body. It's very easy for practitioners of traditional African religions to dramatize their inner psychological life. In spite of the high number of superstitious trappings in African religions, there are also therapeutic methods employed that might be as useful to us today as many of the herbal medicines of the aboriginal shamans have been to modern pharmaceutical companies.

One easy remedy which is often used in African religions is the head cleanse, which consists of pouring cool water in the crown, back and sides of our heads to calm us down and is a practice in many African-diasporic traditions.

Elders who preserve the wisdom traditions in African diasporic religions often advise people that they must protect their heads and there are many legends where heroes and anti-heroes lose their heads due to rage or the madness of love and must undergo great trials in order to purge the evil created by their hot-headedness. These narratives might be both didactically and therapeutically useful.

Protecting our heads is done metaphorically by constantly minding our moods (or, as we like to say, doing "all things as if Epicurus was watching") and choosing to pay attention to only the things that deserve our attention, but it's also done literally via pouring cool water, which feels very soothing, over the head as frequently as needed, in order to keep a cool, controlled head. In African diasporic religions, this is done with prayers and ceremony, but a simpler, philosophical adaptation of this tradition can perhaps be applied prior to meditative practices, prior to sleep, or when we're attacked by fury, in order to facilitate the cooling of the head.

Like the African elders do, I invite my readers to protect your heads, both figuratively and literally. This is one of the most important pieces of advice that Epicurus was trying to convey. I reiterate: we must protect our heads. Please ponder the importance of this in your reasonings.

Philodemus said the less we care about externals, the less anger we have. Anger is dependent on our vulnerabilities and on exposure. Therefore, another way in which we can avoid anger in life is through self-sufficiency, which will be discussed at length in our chapter on autarchy.

New Verbiage:

Argument
Confession
Dispositions
Faith
False Belief
Frank Speech or *Parrhesia*
Head cooling
Hedonic Calculus
Informing
Purging
Rational Anger
Reasonings
Relabeling
Remedy
Suavity

Task: Chant and Be Happy

Epicurean therapy calls for memorization of the teachings, which is why they were imparted as the short adages and proverbs that we find in the Vatican Sayings and in the Principal Doctrines, so that they would be easy to repeat and memorize. The first, and most obvious, Epicurean mantra is the Tetrapharmakon. The Four Remedies read thus:

We do not fear the Gods
We do not fear death
What is good is easy to attain
What is evil is easy to endure

In addition to the adages that are scattered throughout the text of this book, many of the other doctrines in the writings lend themselves to the practices of mantra recitation and chanting. We may choose from among them in order to fully assimilate the teachings:

Death is nothing to us;
for what has disintegrated lacks awareness,
and what lacks awareness is nothing to us.

Natural wealth is both limited and easy to acquire,
but the riches incited by groundless opinion have no end.

One who acts aright is utterly steady and serene,
whereas one who goes astray is full of trouble and confusion.

Friendship dances around the world
announcing to each of us that we must awaken to happiness.

The esteem of others is outside our control;
we must attend instead to healing ourselves.

Nothing is enough to one for whom enough is very little.

The greatest fruit of self-reliance is freedom.

These are all drawn from the above mentioned two texts, and repetitive recitation is a great way to memorize them.

There is also the motto of the Society of Friends of Epicurus, "Do all things as if Epicurus was watching," which introduces an element of internalizing the presence of a guru-figure and cultivating mindfulness of him with the understanding that he embodies all of the philosophical virtues: equanimity, autarchy, cheerfulness, etc. The motto reminds us of our commitment to live a pleasant life, which requires a firm resolution and constant re-dedication. The motto underlines the constant work of self-betterment that applied philosophy constitutes, which is echoed in the following maxim.

One must laugh and seek wisdom and tend to one's home life and use one's other goods, and always recount the pronouncements of true philosophy.
—Vatican Saying 41

Of course, there is no reason to stick to our tradition. So long as chants, mantras and sutras from other traditions do not contradict the tenets of our own, they may be useful means to develop whatever virtues they praise.

References:

Asmis, Elizabeth. "The Necessity of Anger in Philodemus' On Anger," in Fish, Jeffrey & Sanders, Kirk R. (Eds.), *Epicurus and the Epicurean Tradition.* (New York: Cambridge University Press, 2006).

Boggenpoel, Eve. "Om for your health." *Women's Fitness,* May, 2013. Retrieved from http://www.womensfitness.co.uk/health/758/om-your-health

Davies, Nigel. *Human Sacrifice in History and Today.* (New York: William Morrow and Co., 1981) p.54-55.

Moussaieff, Arieh et al. "Incensole acetate, an incense component, elicits psychoactivity by activating TRPV3 channels in the brain." *The FASEB Journal*, April 10, 2008. Retrieved from http://www.fasebj.org/content/22/8/3024

Nussbaum, Martha C. *The Therapy of Desire: Theory and Practice in Hellenistic Ethics.* (Princeton University Press, 1996.)

VI

SCIENCE OF CONTEMPLATION

The practice of meditation helps to release endorphins and research demonstrates that its effects are comparable to the runner's high (Harte, 1995). Research in the field of neuroplasticity also demonstrates that the brain changes within a fairly short span of time as a result of regular meditation (Lazar, 2005). We can easily and scientifically create new neural pathways and train ourselves to experience a natural high with more frequency by engaging in simple, pleasant contemplative disciplines.

Our tradition's epistemology teaches that knowledge can be gained directly from immediate experience and from the senses. One of the results of this ability to directly observe reality is that it emancipates us from traditional and external authorities whenever they contradict the evidence and the firm reality that is observed by the senses. An additional repercussion of this is that knowledge is not merely abstract and cognitive in nature. It can also be sensual.

The Greek word *enargeia*, which translates as "lucidity" and "immediacy of experience," is generally used to refer to an author's ability to conjure up in his reader a sense of full immersion in an experience as if it were real. This is considered the height of the literary arts. It also translates as "evidence." *Enargeia* provides us with a legitimate reason to believe that we are witnessing reality.

However, as it relates to our science of contemplation, *enargeia* can refer to our full, awakened, lucid presence here and now, and should be the goal of an Epicurean meditative practice that is anchored in reality, a contemplative tradition that would no doubt be similar to Buddhist Zen meditation. It is the state of being anchored in the immediacy, in the ordinary, in what the senses are perceiving now. The mind does not wander, the attention is focused and abides here and now.

If philosophy translates as love of wisdom, and if wisdom or knowledge can be acquired not just through cognition but directly and immediately through the senses, then philosophy, to us, is more than just love of science, wisdom traditions, abstract thought, and cognitive knowledge: it is love of reality as experienced directly because the immediacy of (even sensual) experience is also a type of wisdom and knowledge. Philosophy, to us, is also love of reality as it is. It is an affirmation of life and of what is.

In other words, there is a non-cognitive way to know an apple: to taste it. There is a Biblical way to know someone: through love-making. Although reason must never be dismissed, we must accept that it is only one tool for apprehension of reality, that there are more intimate, direct ways of knowing than the cognitive ones and that experience is also a form of knowledge.

It Is What It Is

Enargeia, within the Epicurean theory of contemplation, means saying yes to life and saying no to non-being. It's a refusal to escape into fantasies about the afterlife, to escape into non-reality and into the imaginal (so-called spiritual) realm, in favor of serene, mindful acceptance, even blissful enjoyment, of our immediacy, of nature and things as they are.

There is an insightful Zen saying that I've heard frequently in Chicago which goes "it is what it is." In Zen Buddhism, the non-judgmental presence that is simply mindful of things as they are, without neurotic attachments or aversions, is known as "suchness" or sometimes "thusness." Many Buddhist masters say that a disciplined Zen mind, a Buddha mind, is one that is mindful but has no-mind. It's alert, awake, and pays attention, but is not hypnotized by the perpetual narratives, the tyranny of words and concepts, that the mind is constantly weaving and habituated to. The freedom of mind to gain insights into suchness is always available to us.

Zen meditation was of great use to me some years back. Buddhist teachings on impermanence helped me to cope with both the death of family members and with the loss of a job and subsequent under-employment after the 2008 fiscal crisis.

During *zazen* (sitting meditation), I became mindful of my body and observed the great amount of stress that lodged itself in different parts of my body. I also realized how my uncomfortable sleeping habits created pain. These insights into the habitual state of my body and mind may not seem very important, but they were crucial to the removal of the very toxic levels of stress that I lived with and allowed me to loosen up considerably.

Zen, often described as "just being there," also taught me to become more patient and compassionate with myself and others, to understand and accept more of human nature.

Zen has to do with being rather than doing or thinking. It is the contemplative practice of abiding pleasure, the cultivation of mindfulness in the present moment, of breathing, simply existing without views or opinions. One focuses on the activity that one is doing, even if it's just breathing and sitting. It seems ironic that a so-called state of no-mind helps to liberate us from our habitual mindlessness ... but it is what it is. By stopping the constant narratives that we use to weave reality and block and distort our clear, direct perception of reality as it is, we gain insight into thusness and we easily remain imperturbable, in a state of equanimity and serenity.

On the Benefits of Mindfulness

Normal levels of stress have negligible effects, but the effects of the prevalent high levels of anxiety in the body are considerable and lead to eating and sleeping disorders, heart and immune problems, depression, suicide, and a general lack of existential and physical health (American Psychological Association, 2012).

The non-resolute cannot have a developed consciousness; he has neither happiness or peace. And how can there be any bliss without peace? The reason of a man who yields to the pressure of passions gets carried away as a boat on the water is swept away by a storm.

—Bhagavad Gita 2:66-67

In recent years, Tibetan monks have partnered up with neuroscientists and allowed the scientific study of their brains under scans while they meditate so that there is no shortage of research data available on the effects of meditation. Some of it points to new discoveries in neuroplasticity, which studies how fast the brain changes as a result of meditative practices and other experiences. There are tangible, physical and chemical changes that happen in the brain when we take up the practice of meditation, and they do not take a lifetime or even years to show. Most importantly for the purposes of a hedonic philosophical discipline, we become happier, more relaxed and confident when we take up meditation.

In addition to sitting meditation, there is loving-kindness —or *metta*—meditation whose benefits are considerable, creating a more loving, happy, open, compassionate and blissful mind as the brain releases a feel-good chemical known as oxytocin, which encourages us to trust and feel safe. One Stanford University study concluded that loving-kindness meditation increases social connectiveness (Hutcherson, 2008), and an ancient Buddhist scripture known as the Path of Liberation cites benefits having to do with better quality of sleep. When we are more loving, we also feel safer and become more tolerant and able to engage in empathy, which makes us more likeable. Loving-kindness practice helps to overcome resentment, anger, hatred, and other emotions that produce a hellish existence.

New Verbiage

Enargeia
Loving-kindness Meditation
Mindfulness
Sitting Meditation
Suchness
Thusness

Task: Practice Sitting Meditation

While some may argue that proper practice of *zazen* requires an instructor, I personally learned by reading quite good books on Zen by Japanese masters and by just doing it, sometimes by myself and sometimes in the company of people from my neighborhood Buddhist temple. Many Buddhist temples offer Zen classes and, the more we practice, the better we get.

The basic protocol is as follows:

It helps to stretch, tense and then relax the muscles one by one, and/or take five minutes for deep breathing techniques prior to the exercise so that the body begins to eliminate stress.

Set aside at least 15-20 minutes and find a quiet place for sitting meditation.

Sit in an erect posture. Some people prefer to sit on a cushion and cross their legs, while others prefer a chair. Find your least distracting, most comfortable position. I find that I generally need to sit against a wall or tall chair so that my spine will remain erect.

You may close your eyes, or keep them half-open. Except in cases where there are too many distractions, it is more important to remain mindful than to keep the eyes closed.

Be present. Feel the sensations in the different parts of your body, one by one. And then anchor your attention on the breath, which becomes your tool for focus. Do not seek to control it or deepen it, but simply observe its natural rhythm. Be awake and make no efforts. If you get distracted, simply return to the tide of your breath. Your breath is the song of your life, the eternal companion for as long as you live. Befriending your breath is befriending your life. If you learn to find calm and pleasure in just breathing with no attempts to control it, or your mind or emotions, you will be able to find yourself at ease just by mindfully focusing on the breath.

Allow yourself to settle into tranquility. Some traditions refer to a feeling of being stable like a mountain, while others use the metaphor of the calm lake when there's no agitation.

You will derive the most benefits from meditation if you turn it into a practice, that is, if you do it regularly and develop your own contemplative tradition.

Task: Practice Just Being

A simpler and easier alternative to sitting meditation is to have five minutes of silent being. The mind naturally wants to focus on something, or finds a distraction, so that you should anchor your awareness on your breath. The lower belly is a great place to anchor your breathe and your attention with no effort.

Enjoy simply being. Not thinking, not doing. Discover and master silent, quiet pleasure in just being. Existing pleases you and at that moment, you need or want nothing. You're satisfied. Realize that this is the healthy and natural mood of your organism. Hold that state and that awareness for at least five minutes, twice daily. This is a great exercise for the end of the day.

Task: Practice loving-kindness meditation

The art of loving-kindness meditation is very simple. Prior to it, one may soothe one's mind by deep breathing. Then, for several minutes each, the practice is generally directed at:

oneself
then a friend
then a neutral person
then a difficult person
and then gradually all sentient beings

Most practitioners utilize well-wishing words, such as "May you be happy. May you prosper. May you be at ease. May all beings be safe," etc., as a way to cultivate kindness. The inclusion of yourself in your loving-kindness process helps to understand philosophy as a compassionate attempt to alleviate all suffering, beginning with our own. Become your own friend and cultivate your own resolution to live a pleasant life first. Then develop a friendly disposition to others and help others live pleasant lives. Both attitudes will help beautify your character. Another form of *metta* meditation consists of repeating the mantra:

May all beings
in all the worlds
be eternally happy

You may do it for three, five, or ten minutes. Again, although it appears to be a prayer (and an unanswerable one), the correctly understood purpose of the practice is to cultivate the quality of loving-kindness. The above mantra is inspired by the popular Sanskrit mantra for *metta* meditation *Loka Samastha Sukhino Bhavantu*.

References

American Psychological Association. *How stress affects your health*. (Revised 2013.) Retrieved from http://www.apa.org/helpcenter/stress.aspx

Harte, J. L., Eifert, G. H., and Smith, R. "The effects of running and meditation on beta-endorphin, corticotropin-releasing hormone and cortisol in plasma, and on mood." *PubMed*, June 1995. Retrieved from http://www.ncbi.nlm.nih.gov/pubmed/7669835

Lazar, Sara, Kerr, Catherine, and Fischi, Bruce. "Meditation experience is associated with increased cortical thickness." *Neuroreport*, November 28, 2005. Retrieved from http://www.ncbi.nlm.nih.gov/pmc/articles/PMC1361002/

VII

DEVELOPING YOUR HEDONIC REGIMEN

In our comparisons of dynamic and abiding pleasures, we have learned that abiding pleasure is superior because it does not require externals. Learning how to cultivate it is therefore a major priority in the practice of Epicureanism.

If we are prudent, we understand that even if diverse mood boosters do not have negative side effects, some may be more valuable than others based on their stability and long term effects, while others may have only short term benefits. Therefore, a wise person would invest more time in practices that change neural pathways and produce a happier brain for the long term rather than the short term. Short term remedies are not to be dismissed; they simply have a lesser value. Keep this in mind as you develop your own regimen for a pleasant life ... and have fun while doing it!

With these considerations in mind, let's cheerfully carry out the task of articulating tangible ways to apply the insights that we've gained from both science and Epicurus by preparing for ourselves a regimen of simple pleasures, a program for general long-term wellbeing. Please use the following paragraphs as general guidelines and create your very own hedonic regimen.

Many things are probably missing from my suggested list of simple pleasures, sources of pleasure that are highly personal and subjective. Please consider this chapter only the starting point of your own hedonic wisdom tradition and practice.

Think about the spice of life ... for you, not for anyone else. What things, people and places make you laugh, dance and sing? What is your magic carpet? What allows you to indulge your imagination and find your inner child? What things do you celebrate in your life that most of the world may not understand? Maybe you love architectural tours ... or painting ... or reading science fiction or fantasy books ... science, football, fishing, paintballing, playing with your pet or visiting planetariums and aquariums. Follow your bliss!

Every Day is Thanksgiving Day

In order to fight the habit of paying attention to that which is lacking and which produces craving and desire, one remedy endorsed by both Epicurus and research by social scientists is the daily practice of gratitude: the act of becoming instantly aware that we are blessed.

This might take the form of a gratitude journal, or an inclusion of a daily gratitude portion in our journaling practice. It may also involve a daily act of appreciation: before or after meditation or any of our other practices, we may stop for a minute to ponder what we appreciate that day. Maybe we heard from a friend we haven't heard from in a long time; maybe the health of a loved one is getting better; maybe we are happy to reminisce about good times with one who is gone; maybe we are happy to have a pet or to have an abundance of food or other material goods. Maybe there is good news, or maybe the bad news isn't so bad because we always have a Plan B, and since for every door that closes new ones open, now we're getting excited about the new possibilities. Perhaps we're even grateful for some new technology, or some new music or food we recently discovered.

One way to train ourselves to appreciate what we have is to consider the opposite. Elderly people often praise the health and beauty of youth. If you take for granted the rain and the showers that you take daily, ponder what it's like for people who live in desert regions. If you have loving friends and family members by your side, ponder the isolation that you may have felt at one point and that many people live with daily. There is a huge need for more love in this world.

Ingratitude is a bad habit by which we needlessly punish ourselves. When we no longer have the things we enjoy, we miss them and long for the past, long for what is not there, long to escape. Being always mindfully unhappy and mindlessly happy is not a prudent way to live. The Epicurean must train himself to be mindfully happy.

The practice of gratitude creates the kind of mind that is required for the practice of abiding pleasure. Therefore, make every day Thanksgiving Day.

Minimalist and Simple Living

Frugality and simplicity, like hygiene, are useful virtues to cultivate, particularly if we are scattered and disorganized. It is oftentimes believed—and I tend to concur—that when we live in a disorganized space, our minds are also disorganized. It does not take a *feng shui* practitioner to understand how, in our homes, the outer is an expression of the inner. Many have come to this insight independently. There are entire cultural movements around the idea of minimalism, frugality and simple living.

Sometimes we hold on to things that have no use for reasons of emotional attachment. But stale emotions inhibit fresh experience. It's healthy to create space for new things. Once a year, it might be a good idea to have an eBay sale or a garage sale, to get rid of the excess of things. Things do not make people happy: it is relationships, and a sane mind, that have a true bearing on happiness.

Seasonal cleaning is also therapeutic. Even if I'm physically exhausted from all the work, I generally feel a deep tranquility and clarity of mind after a thorough process of cleaning and getting rid of the excess of useless things. You may increase the pleasure you find in cleaning by listening to your favorite music while you do it and enhancing the aromas in your home through the use of lavender or other fragrances, or incense.

The Home Spa

Hot baths are among the most simple and easy to attain pleasures, and they're good for calming the nerves. They are great if we've had a long day or if the mind is too active and we need to wind down for the night. The art of the hot bath can be easily enhanced with candles, bubbles, salts, or herbs. Alternately, bathing in plain water is just fine.

If done before bed time, drinking sweetened chamomile and linden tea or other mild sedatives may enhance the pre-sleep ritual. Cold baths are advised for the morning, as they wake us up and stimulate us.

Hygiene is a desire necessary for our health, therefore we should turn hygiene into part of our culture of simple pleasures. While it is true that some of these enhancements (the bubble bath rather than a regular one) are considered unnecessary pleasures, Epicurus encourages us to enjoy unnecessary pleasures that have no negative side effects from time to time.

Don't Forget Your Daily Dose of Laughter and Smile

I am about to share here the secret of the most pleasant and auspicious of the natural medicines that the human and simian body and mind can produce (chimpanzees and gorillas also laugh). Everyone has their own unique laughter: consider yours to be the ecstatic song of your soul. Celebrate life! Try using ha-has and tee-hees as mantras, remedies against your life's difficulties and note the effects in your journal.

Laughter therapy, also known as laughter yoga, is empowering: it makes you feel superior to whatever person or situation is making you feel small. People who laugh and smile often are considered more attractive, more confident and fun to be around and they even live longer (Gutman, 2011).

Laughter also lowers blood pressure, reduces stress and pain, and boosts the immune system. Advocates of laughter yoga advise fifteen minutes of deep-belly laughter as the recommended daily dose for general health (University of Maryland, 2005).

Laughter is contagious, so that even if at first you're not tickled, after you've started laughing it will become easier to keep laughing ... and it's also a great gift to give your friends and loved ones, particularly if they're ill or dealing with difficulties. Become a jester! Find ways to make those you care about laugh!

By the same token, find the people in your life that easily make you laugh and resolve to seek their company more frequently. There are people who easily bring laughter into every room they enter, into every relationship they build. Some Native American cultures understand that laughter is medicine and consider clowns to be sacred people whose mission is to make sure members of the community don't take themselves too seriously (Andreas, 1995). Those gifted with clowning can easily lighten our loads and are always good allies on the path to a pleasant life.

The Foods of the Gods

Let food be your medicine. —Hippocrates

There is a beautiful verse in the *Dhammapada* (The Gospel of the Buddha) that says "Let us live feeding on joy, like the bright Gods." Epicurus, similarly, said that the goal of philosophy is to make us blissful like the gods ... and that pleasure starts in the stomach. It is no accident that the metaphor for paradise is traditionally that of a garden of delights: many of our favorite delicacies, fruits, teas and aromatic herbs that season and make whatever we cook much more opulent, come from nature and are found in gardens.

It is perhaps in the kitchen that we are able to derive the most pleasure out of our most universal necessary desire and where we can easily understand how the things that are pleasant are also good for us, and how the things that are good for us also bring pleasure. We have evolved a tongue and a nose that are the precise tools for sensing the flavors that fulfill our dietary requirements.

We can also use our choice of simple delicacies as a way to enhance the chemical cocktail that the brain must concoct in order for us to be happy. We know that the brain needs tryptophan in order to synthesize serotonin, the feel-good chemical, which is also instrumental in improving the quality of sleep. Here are some of the delicacies that contain tryptophan:

- egg whites
- the superfood spirulina
- kelp and other seaweeds
- Atlantic cod
- salmon
- soy beans, raw or sprouted
- sesame seeds
- cheese and yoghurt
- meats
- mangos
- dates
- bananas
- durian

Notice that seaweeds are usually lacking in the American diet, but are a dietary staple in Japan where people on average have longer life spans than in the US. Spirulina is not to everyone's liking, but I've found spirulina energy bars that were quite tasty and discovered that the strong smell and flavor of spirulina powder can be easily masked by adding it into a mashed avocado.

I have developed an easy and adaptable recipe for seaweed soup that uses miso stock as its base, and which I consume on average every week or every other week. There are many variations of it: I've used rice noodles, sticky rice, or other noodles; I've made it with or without oyster mushrooms, broccoli and bean sprouts. These are usually first stir-fried in teriyaki or soy sauce, garlic and sofrito (a Latin American spice mix). I've even added goji berries to the soup.

I always have several varieties of seaweeds which can easily be soaked in water for ten minutes to make a soup that I've always found to have calming effects. Not much seaweed is needed, as it expands in water, and it's ridiculously inexpensive. One bag of seaweed may cost less than two dollars at an Asian market and last me for months, and miso paste can last up to a year, which makes my seaweed soup one of the most simple, nutritionally rich and inexpensive pleasures in my hedonic regimen.

You may have your own comfort foods similar to my seaweed soup. Why not add ingredients that promote happiness? I frequently add maca powder to my yoghurt or almond milk. Maca is a super-food: an adaptogen that resets our hormonal system and helps to fight stress. It tastes malty and creamy.

Of all the foods that nature has given us, none is more beneficial to a blissful, happy existence than raw cacao. It is a mineral-rich anti-depressant, great for the brain, and contains anandamide—which literally translates as "the chemical of bliss." Anandamide is what the brain produces when we experience the runner's high, or when we reach an orgasm. Anandamide is also present in most commercial chocolate, but its beneficial effects are dwarfed by all the added sugar. The ancient Mayans were on to something when they considered chocolate the food of the gods and used cacao beans as currency. Don't forget to add a small dose of raw cacao to your pleasure regimen!

In addition to raw chocolate bars, you may prepare chocolate and maca beverages with almond milk (or chilled coconut water) and a sweetener. If you'd like to make raw ice cream, place a frozen banana in the blender with all the previously mentioned ingredients and experience heaven with no guilt.

Foods high in Omega 3 oils are important for over-all health but particularly for the health of the brain. They fight anxiety and fatigue, and are found in the following foods:

- salmon, halibut, tuna and other fish and fish oils
- milk and its by-products
- soy beans
- spinach, kale, Brussels sprouts, and other greens
- juice
- flaxseed, walnuts, pumpkin seeds, peanuts, and other nuts and nut oils
- oatmeal and cereal

Some mood boosters, in addition to being natural stimulants (like yerba maté) or relaxants (like kava or some teas), also afford us with a sense of ceremony and ritual which can be utilized in private or in the company of good friends.

Yerba maté, known as the drink of friendship, became one of my favorites after I overcame caffeine addiction some years back. It is a sweetened herbal drink that comes from South America and can be enjoyed cold as a tereré (a Paraguayan herbal lemonade) or hot in its traditional gourd (known as a maté), which is passed around among friends in the same manner that friends share the pipe of peace.

In many Pacific isles, kava is a traditional island beverage used in ceremonies, to mark weddings, and to reconcile enemies. Also known as the drink of peace—or grog—it is a pungent, peppery root which is sold in the form of a powder, steeped in water for about twenty minutes, passed through a cheese cloth, and served in a *bilo* or coconut shell that is shared among friends. Although it tastes like mud, it produces a mild high where the muscles are relaxed but the mind is alert and it's enjoyed for the after-effects. Many of the proponents of kava see it as a natural alternative to synthetic pharmaceutical products that fight anxiety. I simply drink it for the pleasure it gives me.

Epicureanism proposes that necessary desires, like the need for food, enjoy a place of priority in our pleasure regimen. Modern science has tools at its disposal that allow us to identify foods that enhance our well-being, health and happiness. The ancient Epicurean school could not have had access to these modern tools, but would have considered them of great practical use if they had been available because they enhance our scientific understanding of happiness and their application is easy to put into practice. For these reasons, although the specific comfort foods, superfoods and mood boosters that I mention here fall within the category of unnecessary desires, by virtue of their health benefits there is much reason to implement their use to fulfill our necessary desire for food.

Not all people find pleasure in cooking and preparing dishes. It's advisable to learn to enjoy the simple pleasures of not just consuming, but also preparing food, because so much of our time must be dedicated to the necessary pleasure of eating. One way to enhance this practice is to gather our ancestral recipes, and those that we learn along the way as we seek to develop a more mindful lifestyle, into recipe books or collections. If your recipes contain comfort foods, super-foods and mood-boosters, this culinary folklore has the added value of being already part of your very own Epicurean wisdom tradition. Name it and celebrate it!

Make Love

Sex is a great way to easily induce the brain to secrete endorphins and other feel-good chemicals. Endorphins are the body's own private narcotic: neurotransmitters that have the ability to produce analgesia (immunity to pain) and a feeling of well-being. They also reduce stress and anxiety, fight depression, and improve the quality of sleep. There are many varieties of endorphins. Beta-endorphins are particularly potent: they are stronger than morphine.

One of the components of ataraxia is *aponia*, or lack of physical pain. Because endorphins help with pain reduction, activities that increase endorphin-production are useful when we are in physical pain. If we become familiar with what activities contribute to the release of endorphins, we can develop a more scientific approach to our pursuit of *aponia* and of happiness. In addition to love-making, these activities include exercise and sports. Eating hot peppers also produces a flood of endorphins (Yao, 2009).

Studies suggest that both acupuncture and massage therapy can stimulate endorphin secretion. This may have to do with our need for tactile interaction and affection. Notice, again, our closest relatives: chimpanzees and other apes very diligently groom each other and reassure each other constantly. Physical interaction and affection generates a sense of safety and security that Epicurus pointed out as one of the benefits of having lots of friends. Therefore, always remember that friends are for hugging!

As for the desire for sexual love, it's considered natural but not necessary. It can add to our pleasure but we should not need it. We should be confident that we can be happy with or without it. In Vatican Saying 51, advice is given to a young man who has strong sexual inclinations to follow his inclination as long as it's not a source of perturbances. Among potential perturbances there is mention of violating the laws, harming neighbors, injuring one's body, and wasting one's possessions. An added potential difficulty not mentioned here is sexually transmitted diseases, for most of which there are methods of avoidance. The adage then concludes that "a man never gets any good from sexual passion, and he is fortunate if he does not receive harm." And so here prudence, again, is queen of all virtues.

If the above mentioned young man decided that his passion for someone was leading him to lose his possessions, his mind, or his health, and that he wished to sever the connection with the source of his perturbance, Vatican Saying 18 advises the remedy of removal from the association of the object of one's desires: "The passion of love disappears without the opportunity to see each other and talk and be together."

Exercise

There are few mood boosters as efficient as exercise. I find that a daily run, even if for less than half an hour, can have great effects on my state of mind all day, particularly if I jog early in the morning.

The "runner's high," a natural euphoria that athletes experience when they push their bodies to the limit, is known to be caused by the release of endorphins as the body attempts to alleviate the pain of strenuous physical exercise. If you run or exercise during a sunny day, you may also acquire a sunny disposition as a result of exposure to the sun.

Several years ago I experimented with the Brazilian martial art of *capoeira*, which is a combination of fighting, dancing, music, and exercise. I remember experiencing a natural high for days after each 90-minute session so that even though my legs ached for about five days after exercising, I enjoyed the feeling and felt like I was on top of the world. The addition of trance-like songs and the camaraderie that one finds in a martial arts school made the *capoeira* experience even more ecstatic. Other sports are likely to confer similar effects.

Get Rest and Meditate

I have already covered meditation in a previous chapter, but a word must be said about the need for rest. In order to avoid exhaustion, we must get enough sleep and avoid scattering our energies in too many directions. Generally, an eight hour sleep is enough for most people.

Lack of sleep contributes to heart problems, depression and mood swings, makes it difficult to focus, and decreases productivity at work. Some people use caffeine-free teas as sleep aids (chamomile and linden are my favorite combination). Others take a hot bath, play relaxing music or meditate. You should use whatever aids the quality of your sleep.

The Therapy of Journaling

I've always found pleasure in journaling or in the more modern, less intimate art of blogging. By putting our thoughts down on paper, we glean clarity as to what we really want and what we truly feel. We are more clear-headed when we make our decisions after careful journaling, which is also an excellent tool for living the analyzed life.

Also, if we wish to approach happiness as a science, we must first of all understand that all science requires experiments and that the experimental process requires careful observation and note-taking. By journaling about our process of flourishing, we can develop a more or less scientific approach to the pursuit of happiness and well-being, and it helps to keep track of our progress.

References

Andreas, Peggy. *Path of the Sacred Clown*. Dreamflesh.com, 1995. Retrieved from http://dreamflesh.com/essays/clown-path/

Gutman, Ron. "The hidden power of smiling." [Video, 2011]. Retrieved from http://www.youtube.com/watch?v=U9cGdRNMdQQ

Hutcherson, Cendri A. *et al.* (2008). "Loving-Kindness Meditation Increases Social Connectedness." *Emotion*, Vol. 8, No. 5 (2008). Retrieved from http://spl.stanford.edu/pdfs/Hutcherson_08_2.pdf

University of Maryland. "School of Medicine Study Shows Laughter Helps Blood Vessels Function Better." University of Maryland Medical Center, March 7, 2005. Retrieved from http://umm.edu/news-and-events/news-releases/2005/school-of-medicine-study-shows-laughter-helps-blood-vessels-function-better#ixzz2Zocf47xG

VIII

THE TREASURE OF FRIENDSHIP

Of all the things which wisdom provides to make us entirely
happy, much the greatest is the possession of friendship.
—Epicurus

Friendship is the main ingredient in human happiness. Harvard psychologist and happiness researcher Dan Gilbert confirms Epicurus' insights on how meaningful relations significantly increase the amount of pleasure and of memorable experiences that we gather throughout our lifetime (Wilkinson, 2012). Friends considerably increase our simple pleasures, and greatly decrease our suffering. It's much easier to bear our difficulties with loyal friends, and they also make watching a movie, partaking of a meal, sports and other activities much more enjoyable.

It is not so much our friends' help that helps us, as
the confidence of their help.
—Epicurus

In our tradition, friends serve as a kind of insurance against difficulties. They strengthen our Epicurean identity and provide familiarity, security, safety, and protection from hostility. When I submitted an online survey to my Epicurean acquaintances (some of whom are very active on the "Garden of Epicurus" group on Facebook) asking them to choose what we should name ourselves, the majority voted for the word Friends. Hence, among Epicureans, the word Friend is used almost as a title and not just as a common noun.

Other wisdom traditions from various cultures around the world also teach the importance of wholesome association, which is known as *satsang* in Hinduism. Catholics speak of the "communion of saints" and Buddhists consider the *sangha* (the community of beings seeking enlightenment) as one of the three refuges. One Yoruba proverb states that "One tree does not a forest make."

Ancient Scandinavians were among the peoples for whom friendship was sacred. The *Havamal*, which serves in part as a recollection of ancestral wisdom, advises frequent association and blending of minds with true friends, loyalty, and gifts exchange as a way of sealing and honoring friends, and even singing together with abandon in exuberant celebration of life's most precious gift: friendship.

> Young was I once, I walked alone,
> and bewildered seemed in the way;
> then I found me another and rich I thought me,
> for man is the joy of man.
>
> If you have a friend in whom you trust,
> seek him often;
> For brambles grow and waving grass
> on untrodden paths.
>
> Attract good-natured men to you with happy runes,
> sing songs of joy while you live.
>
> Be not quick to break the bond of love for your friend;
> Sorrow will rend the heart
> If you dare not tell another your whole mind.
> —*Havamal*, Stanzas 47, 118-120

Wisdom traditions often evolve within the context of friends seeking advice from those most trusted among them. They invariably incorporate practical wisdom about the ability to discern between true and false friends, which has always been among the most important life lessons mortals must learn. Stanza 43 of the *Havamal* warns that any person who befriends your foes cannot be considered a true friend. On the other hand, the friends of your friends are also your friends. It is true that friends help to extend our circles of trust and familiarity: it's usually easier to trust the people that our best friends trust.

> The pine tree wastes which is perched on the hill,
> nor bark nor needles shelter it;
> such is the man whom none doth love;
> for what should he longer live?
>
> —*Havamal*, Stanza 50

If friendship is an Epicurean remedy, then perhaps we should articulate what the disease consists of. Isolation increases suffering. The reason for so many evils tied to loneliness may have to do with how it's a source of stress, which is a risk factor for many mental and physical conditions. According to research by Goldman (2006), isolation is a risk factor for disease on par with smoking and obesity. One University of Chicago study even found that isolation could increase cancerous tumor growth (Cozen, Suzanne D. et al., 2009).

In America there's an epidemic of isolation. John Cacioppo, of the University of Chicago, found that 20 percent of all people are unhappy because of social isolation at any given moment. The wisdom writings of the Bible also celebrate friendship.

> *Two are better than one, because they have a good reward*
> *for their toil. For if they fall, one will lift up his fellow; but*
> *woe to him who is alone when he falls and has not another*
> *to lift him up. Again, if two lie together, they are warm;*
> *but how can one be warm alone?*
>
> —Ecclesiastes 4:9-11

Interestingly, the Association for Psychological Science has published research that demonstrates that solitude literally feels cold (Zhong & Leonardelli, 2008). There are physical, bodily repercussions to loneliness.

Happiness is contagious: when we are happy we make others happy, and are more productive and responsible citizens (Christakis, 2008). The cultivation of our own happiness can therefore be understood as a public service.

Dr. Nicholas Christakis authored a 20-year-long Harvard Medical School study on how social networks affect a person's happiness and found that even happy people who are two or three degrees removed from us can positively affect our happiness. Unhappy friends also make us unhappier. It seems that, as social animals, we act like a school of fish and mirror each other's behaviors and attitudes even on a very subtle level. Our choice of friends becomes, therefore, crucial to our happiness.

Not only was Dr. Christakis able to attach percentages of added chances of (un)happiness per (un)happy friend; he was also able to compare the research results with previous studies that linked happiness to wealth and boldly capitalized friendship by saying that "a happy friend is worth about $20,000." What an auspicious currency! This insight of how there can be social currencies should change our wealth paradigm.

The image that emerges is one of a circle, or perhaps a chain of happy friends around each happy person. Equipped with this knowledge, we can then strategize on how to seek more frequent association with the happy people in our lives and, just as importantly, to be a happier presence for others.

While not all of us are eager to attach monetary value to our friends, there is another currency in which they're valuable and esteemed: time. They are our chosen people during a limited time on earth. We are free to associate with anyone, as free agents, while we're here and we have the conviction that there is only this one life. Therefore, time is not to be wasted. The time that we waste will never be recovered. If we have this understanding, by making a choice to spend our very limited time on earth in the company of our chosen friends, we are giving them a precious non-renewable resource: our time. We are investing something in our friends that we will never regain. We should therefore carefully and consciously choose our associations and nurture our covenants of friendship.

Furthermore, each friend is a unique being with a unique history. We may think of each friend as an adventure through which unique things can be known and unique experiences can be had. No one can replicate or replace a true friend.

The Rules of Philosophical Friendship

The nature of Epicurean therapy is such that it calls for mutual correction. In the ongoing process of self-betterment and healing moral disease, we are called to blend our minds with each other and work through our fears, anger, and other undesirable emotions with the help of others who are on the same path.

We are called to engage in *parrhesia*, a Greek word which translates as "frank speech." According to Norman DeWitt, who authored *Organization and Procedure in Epicurean Groups*, it was considered lack of fidelity for a friend to not be honest with another friend, regardless of how candid or harsh the criticism may be. As a result of the dynamics of mutual correction and frank speech, which must have created awkward situations, Epicureans had to learn the art of suavity in order to sweeten their frank speech.

Frank speech was not employed, as in some communist societies, as a means to humiliate people. It was known that Epicurus did not look kindly upon the use of sophistry by other schools of philosophy to humiliate and degrade pupils. On the contrary, kindly telling the truth was meant to be therapeutic and helpful. In his work *On Frank Speech*, Philodemus said:

Frank speech is the sole nourishment suitable for the pupil.

The Importance of Inter-Subjectivity

Insistence on friendship as a value and a good, and as

the ideal human form of interaction, also serves to promote subject-subject relations rather than subject-object. This is a prominent concern in Sartrean philosophy, for instance, where the gaze of the other objectifies, represents an exertion of power, and creates tension.

Although there was a clear asymmetry of roles in the original form of Epicurean therapy, the relationship was entered into voluntarily and the process of blending minds and engaging in philosophical discourse evolved into a deep, loving relationship and produced loyalties that lasted a lifetime. It is difficult to imagine these loyalties emerging if there hadn't been respect for the intelligence of the patients, who had at least the intellectual stamina to engage in the process of philosophy and were, therefore, at least moderately smart men and women.

One of the key ingredients for this dynamic of deep friendship to emerge when the roles were not between equals must have been a healthy dose of respect for elders, sages, and those wiser and more experienced than oneself. This is a theme that I will address elsewhere in this book, as it pertains to the value that we attach to wisdom and to wisdom traditions.

This is not an unimportant matter. An uncalculated hedonism easily sees others as objects and degenerates into selfish manipulation of others. A responsible hedonist philosopher, on the other hand, must recognize others as free agents whose dignity, concerns, and interests elicit our compassion and responsibility.

Epicurus' gospel of peace and happiness includes the convenient and accurate observation that friends are one of the most important sources of pleasure, safety, value and joy in human life, and ergo friendship should be sought for its own sake as non-different from pleasure. In this sense, friends are a valuable treasure and every Epicurean must accept the task of learning the art of earning and cultivating wholesome friendships with other subjects.

New Verbiage

Frank Speech
Mutual Correction
Suavity

Task: Develop and Cultivate your Circles of Friends

Now that you understand the importance of having happy friends and philosopher friends, develop a formal plan to daily enhance your network of friends. Honor the friends you have by exchanging gifts and attempt to gain new friends.

If you have friends who may have an interest in philosophy, share this book or other Epicurean material with them as a token of friendship and engage them in philosophical discourse. Have gatherings on the 20th in order to evaluate the merits of Epicurean doctrine.

References

Cacioppo, John T. *Loneliness: Human Nature and the Need for Social Connection*. (New York: W. W. Norton & Company, 2009).

Christakis, Nicholas and Fowler, James. "Dynamic spread of happiness in a large social network: longitudinal analysis over 20 years in the Framingham Heart Study." *British Medical Journal*, 2008. Retrieved from http://www.ncbi.nlm.nih.gov/pmc/articles/PMC2600606/

DeWitt, Norman. *Organization and Procedure in Epicurean Groups*. (The University of Chicago Press, 1936).

Goleman, Daniel. *Emotional Intelligence*. (New York: Bantam, 2006).

Wilkinson, Will. "Invest in Memorable Social Experience." *Big Think*, April 26, 2012. Retrieved from http://bigthink.com/the-moral-sciences-club/invest-in-memorable-social-experience

Williams, J. Bradley *et al*. "A Model of Gene-Environment Interaction Reveals Altered Mammary Gland Gene Expression and Increased Tumor Growth following Social Isolation." *Cancer Prevention Research*, October, 2009. Retrieved from http://cancerpreventionresearch.aacrjournals.org/content/2/10/850.abstract?sid=c8434f64-f1ec-4b14-ae72-18e7183f57b0

Zhong, Chen-Bo and Leonardelli, Geoffrey J. "Cold and Lonely: Does Social Exclusion Literally Feel Cold?" *Association for Psychological Science*, 2008. Retrieved from http://www2.hawaii.edu/~bergen/ling441/coldandlonely.pdf

IX

AUTARCHY

Autarchy (from αὐταρχία, "state of self-rule"), understood as self-sufficiency, self-control, personal sovereignty and independence, is what distinguishes a parasitical hedonic fool who can't control his senses or his desires from a mature, prudent philosopher. A monarch bears the huge burden of ruling his kingdom and his responsibilities are innumerable, whereas an autarch happily rules himself and his affairs and his responsibilities are relatively easy to manage.

Epicurean doctrine teaches that autarchy is one of the Three Goods. In other words, just as we should not depend on externals for our subjective or inner happiness, in the same way it is more desirable to be fiscally independent rather than live at the mercy of others. Both inner and outer attitudes of self-sufficiency are an integral part of the principle of autarchy.

Robert LeFevre, a self-proclaimed autarchist, has created a libertarian political theory which he has labeled autarchy and which is influenced by ancient philosophy. However, Epicurus advised his followers to "Live unknown" and to be apolitical. Political involvement, he believed, breeds intrigue, has a corrupting effect on the character and is detrimental to our serenity.

Therefore, although Thomas Jefferson was an engaged Epicurean and was involved in political life, Epicurus' doctrine on autarchy was specifically non-political and contemporary political theories of autarchy, which may or may not have merit, are modern evolutions of an ancient idea. In this book I am not concerned with the libertarian ideals that were, in part, inspired by Epicurus but with fleshing out the philosophical theory and practice of self-reliance. I'm concerned with how Epicurus taught it, how his followers applied it, and how it can be applied today.

Money: A Natural and Necessary Desire

Let's begin from the beginning. We must apply to money the same criteria that we apply to all desires. In our society, it is undeniable that money is a necessary desire. It provides safety and security, and the fear of not having money is a legitimate one.

A Princeton University study of Gallup data on wealth versus happiness concluded that the emotional benefits of having wealth peak when one reaches an annual income of $75,000, and then may deteriorate from there based on several factors, among them isolation and health. This means that any wealth that one may wish to acquire beyond that threshold is to be considered a vain desire that can be easily dismissed, and perhaps even constitute more of a burden than a boon. For instance, people who are extremely wealthy oftentimes cannot know with certainty whether the loyalties of certain friends depend on the material benefits gained from the friendship.

In our society, the vain desire for excessive amounts of money and displays of wealth have created high levels of debt, as well as petty and violent crime. In addition to this, many people who live in poverty have to subject themselves to abusive and exploitative bosses, bad working conditions, and a general lifestyle of stress all week only to conclude the social Friday by inebriating the stress to oblivion, and then spend the weekend recovering and dreading the following Monday.

The problem of debt (and the consumerism it feeds on) leads to the problem of slavery. These two used to be one and the same. In ancient societies, a person who was unable to pay his debt had to work as a slave for the person to whom he was indebted until his debt was paid in full. There has always been a blurry boundary between debt and slavery. High levels of debt today translate into indentured slavery where people work to pay the powerful banking cartel. It is for this reason that debt is a primary concern if we are to apply Epicurean teachings in our lives. There can be no autarchy, no self-sufficiency and freedom, until one is free from debt.

If we are wage slaves and must have two or three jobs and never have time to spend with friends, to engage in the analyzed life, and to do the things that give us pleasure, it's unlikely that philosophy, the arts, and the most refined civilization will flourish in our midst. Wage slavery is not compatible with a life of philosophy, which requires leisure.

What does philosophy have to say about wage slavery (defined broadly, for our purposes, as over-working or unhappily working without having a choice), and what long-term remedies does it offer?

Throughout philosophical materialism, one of the threads connecting the various traditions is the basic recognition that human beings, in order to live a life of dignity, require meeting their basic needs first; that without food, shelter, time for association with others, etc., human life becomes miserable and inhumane and that ethical discourse must address these basic needs. Epicurus speaks of necessary desires, those without which we experience pain, and developed a theory of inner revolution whereby we eliminate the need for externals and fortify our souls against consumerism and dependence. Marx developed a theory of social revolution, and later Sartre, while committed to freedom, was forced to explore the issue of how we are bound by our facticity, by the things we cannot change.

In addition to the above considerations, we must concede that if a man is to live a life of seeking pleasure for its own sake without balancing the pursuit of pleasure by prudence, he will become lazy, selfish, unreliable, and probably dependent on others.

Autarchy requires an entrepreneurial spirit which was in evidence in the ancient Gardens. Beyond being oases of pleasure, they also served to help philosophers produce their own food. They were made useful. The scribes also made a living from the teaching mission, charging fees for lectures and classes, as well as for the scrolls that they replicated by hand.

The Gardens were, in addition to schools, publishing ventures. Scribes relied on donations and alms, just as any modern non-profit organization would, but they sought the greatest degree possible of self-reliance.

The art of self-sufficiency has the side effect of greatly increasing the value of the things that we do have, even if they're simple and few. Over the years, I have brewed my own beer and kombucha, and I have a soymilk maker which I use frequently to make almond milk. These activities turn water and a few other ingredients into drinks of great value. I have also begun to grow mint, chilis and moringa from branches and seeds given to me by friends.

The Epicurean theory of success is not based on acquisition of goods or amassing wealth, but based on how pleasant we make our existence. Epicurean success lies not in externals, except where it concerns natural and necessary desires.

While money isn't a bad thing, the unhealthy greed and anxiety that people experience because of it are unpleasant and evil. Therefore, the goal of the autarch is to have tranquility without monetary worries for today or for the future. The practical goals that must be met are to secure both the necessary amount of money and the necessary tranquility of mind with regards to wealth. This is done in several ways.

One way is by having the right view on the use and purpose of money as a tool, an object, a means and not an end. We do not live for money. It exists for our sake, as a tool for exchange.

Another way is by having the right view of wealth. We should be cognizant of the ways in which we're already wealthy and of the forms of wealth that require no money. Our friends are a form of wealth. So is the sun, the water we drink, the air we breathe. Our families and communities are wealth. The natural resources all around us are wealth. Time is wealth, and so is all the food we eat. We do not need a deed that shows ownership to be able to fully enjoy these things. We are drowning daily in nature's abundance.

Another way to ensure tranquility and freedom from fiscal worries is by planning for a rainy day, by ensuring our many streams of income meet our current and future needs and by setting a strong foundation in terms of career and savings.

If we don't love what we do, we should establish a strategy to shift careers. If we're interested in self-employment, we may want to minimize the risk of our entrepreneurial ventures by initially doing the work on a part-time basis. We should know the right people and seek successful mentors who can show us the ropes.

In practical terms, the ideal of autarchy requires both the autonomy to be ourselves and the ability to make a comfortable living. Walking daily into a work environment that kills our souls, or where we do not earn sufficiently, is depressing. Authenticity and affluence are part of the balancing act of the autarch.

After pondering the ill fate of several wealthy and powerful rulers and comparing it with the good fortune of an honest and happy gardener who lived off the land in Turkey, the protagonist of Voltaire's Candide concludes:

"All that is very well, but let us cultivate our garden."

Unlike the wage slave, an autarch has a choice in how he will be productive, or else he is not truly free. Even if he develops a steady and stable method for earning a living that feels at times monotonous, there is an awareness of choice. He enjoys what he does or, put another way, he does what pleases him.

Autarchy can be broadly understood as the art of administering our life in its entirety, including fiscal, volitional, psychological, relational and existential needs, and it calls for a practice of constant self-betterment.

Epicurean Ethics of Labor

Philosophers and sages have always discussed the acceptable ways of making a living as a natural extension of conversations about virtue, duty and the good. Different schools offered various criteria for discerning between wholesome and unwholesome professions.

These are many ancient professions that no longer exist, and modern ones that were not in existence in antiquity, so that modern Epicureans must engage in an assessment of what these ancient criteria translate into for our society, and propose their own idealizations of what autarchy looks like in our day and context.

When we consider Philodemus' choices of wholesome ways to make a living, several criteria emerge by which we may judge our contemporary paradigm of labor and our available options. Let this be our starting point in what should be an ongoing conversation about how good Epicureans can earn their wealth today.

Philodemus argued that the philosopher will not choose military or political life, horsemanship, or cultivate the lands with his own hands. He may employ labor, however, to cultivate his land, accept rent from tenants or profit from his slaves as long as exploitation isn't cruel. For instance, Philodemus thought that employing slaves for work in mines was exploitative and unbecoming of a sage. The ideal way to earn a living was through the profession of teaching philosophy, as long as this was done in a spirit of equanimity and not one of intellectual arrogance.

We may conclude, firstly, that physical exploitation and cruelty is unpleasant and that we should not participate in any work environment that is harsh or hellish. Like military service, work in a slaughterhouse, for instance, is the type of work where one may be perturbed by constant day-to-day killing of sentient beings.

Several of Philodemus' acceptable ways of earning a living suggest that we are encouraged to earn residual income by owning means of production. In his examples, slave labor was among the options available. Creating and managing jobs for others via our business ventures is a modern equivalent. The admission of rent from tenants implies that ownership of real estate is another tried-and-true way to gain self-sufficiency.

We are living in times where there is a severe need to reinvent labor. Not only are jobs going to other countries: machines are replacing humans. They are becoming the cashiers in our supermarkets, they are the cash dispensers at our banks, they are answering our phones when we call most major companies (if we are not using online self-service). Each one of the 24-hour automated machines that corporations employ replaces three full-time around-the-clock jobs. Can this be an opportunity? How can we use automation in our favor in a sustainable people's economy?

Curiously, the original meaning of the word "robot" was slave. Automated machines were meant to perform slave labor and the original, altruistic idea of robotics was to emancipate humans and other animals from exploitative or monotonous labor.

When we employed cars, trucks and cranes to replace the oxen, horses and other animals that we had enslaved, this was a major advancement in terms of ending cruelty against the other species. But now that machines are replacing people and the population is growing, and with it poverty and unemployment, this generates a serious problem of shortage of jobs that affects our ability to live with dignity. Many non-traditional systems of sustainable economy, such as time banks and alternative currencies, are emerging to fill the fiscal needs of the progressively larger groups of people that find themselves economically marginalized in our day.

The mechanization of labor, in an ideal world, should increase ordinary people's ability and opportunities to become self-sufficient and to own multiple means of production. It should create the opportunity to reimagine an economy where traditional labor takes up less of our time, where less money is needed, and where ordinary people can easily procure multiple streams of income in order to survive. This, I would argue, should not be seen as a sign of instability but as a remedy against the tediousness of the old model of nine-to-five labor.

Louis Kelso, in his books *The Capitalist Manifesto* and *Two-Factor Theory*, presented a practical economic vision of a world where the physical means of production are broadly owned by ordinary people rather than being owned by either the government or the wealthy few, thus freeing millions for a life of constructive leisure.

Futurists, like Jacques Fresco, have also begun to imagine a future world economy of this sort. But one need not be a dreamer: there are practical reasons to reinvent labor. The failure to pragmatically address the shortage of employment opportunities in an increasingly mechanized world will inevitably produce social unrest.

Philodemus' idealization of the philosophical profession indicates that this was, and should be, the ideal way to make a living and that teachers deserve a fee. The Society of Friends of Epicurus is committed to the belief that being an Epicurean Guide should be one of several legitimate streams of income for contemporary philosophers, just as it was in antiquity, and that elders and people who share the wealth of wisdom in our society should be highly regarded and should have the opportunity to earn a living wage while doing so.

The Spirituality of Autarchy: a Philosophy of Freedom

Freedom is the greatest fruit of self-sufficiency.
—Epicurus

The moral imperative of fiscal self-sufficiency is important for the survival and preservation of the body, its health and safety; but the spiritual ideals of freedom are important for the soul, for happiness and for being able to choose and to create a pleasant life.

The notion that our cosmos has no inherent meaning or purpose is a source of anxiety for Platonic thinkers whose feet are not grounded on reality. But to we who firmly reject the false doctrine of pre-determinism, the challenges presented by our freedom are at the root of Epicureanism's redemptive quality: we are free to create and assign value and meaning through the noble tool of philosophy. We embrace this freedom as liberating and empowering, and we understand that as agents it is inevitable that we will use, knowingly or not, our freedom to co-create our world ... even if we exert our freedom to remain enslaved. Choices, choices, choices!

If we have a clear and lucid understanding of the detrimental spiritual repercussions of denying our freedom, we will naturally develop a firm resolution to gain the crown of autarchy. Determinism and fatalism (the fear of or belief in fate) represent, fundamentally, a denial of our responsibility on the one hand, and a denial of reality on the other hand. We are always free and responsible within the limits of our context and our facticity, within the limits set by biology and, to some extent, society.

Contrast the maturity of freedom-affirming philosophy with how traditional, organized religion treats grown people as children. Among the most prominent examples of this we find that women are not "allowed" to drive and apostates are executed in Saudi Arabia, and that sexual minorities are today still denied the right to marry in many states and countries. Matrimony is seen in most societies as a rite of passage into the responsibilities of adulthood and is even claimed as a sacrament by many religious groups. There are clearly psychological and social changes that are produced when the community honors the marriage of a couple via ceremony. In most societies, getting a license and being able to drive a car is another type of initiation into adult responsibilities.

The denial of access to these rites of passage sends a message to sexual minorities and women that they are not fit to cross the initiatory threshold into adulthood. When the only justification for this denial is state-sponsored false religious doctrine, this raises the question of illegitimate and unnatural power of the state and of religious tyrants over our lives.

We are proud to stress the fact that a female was perfectly acceptable as a pupil among the Epicureans from the very onset, whereas the other schools of philosophy were too uncomfortable with the idea of female philosophers to accept them as pupils. As for the Christians, we know what they did to the philosopher Hypatia: a mob of them murdered her for refusing to convert. I do not know of any other philosophical school this early in history that did not practice gender segregation. The Canon, by allowing us to immediately and directly apprehend reality through our senses and our pain/pleasure principles, emancipates us from traditional "authorities" and gives us the power to discern truth independently. Anyone who can see, touch, feel the objects studied is able to judge in what way these objects are real.

False philosophies can be as detrimental to our dignity and emancipation as false religions. Some, like Stoicism, affirm divine providence and lend themselves to affirming the inevitability of certain constricting (social class, etc.) roles as natural when they are only the product of cultural corruption. This is no different from how Hinduism endorses the caste system. Divine or so-called natural predetermination is invariably useful to whoever is in power.

It is impossible to flourish within a castrating value system that will not recognize when we are not children anymore. We need a philosophy for mature adults, not fables and false consolations for children. The persistent attacks on our freedoms, still today, by adherents of false religions and doctrines eloquently makes the case for the need for a scientific ethics for free adult men and women.

The fact that Epicurus recognizes autarchy as a good indicates that we're on the right track if we are seeking to flourish as intelligent, responsible adults. By being both responsible and creative autarchs, we are in effect making ourselves worthy of the noble tradition that dignifies us in this manner and crowns our heads with this wisdom.

As autonomous value-creating communities, the Epicurean Gardens may one day become spaces where people perform rites of passage according to their authentic needs and informed choices. This would include not only commitment ceremonies and other coming-of-age rites of passage and funerals, but also conversions and passage into higher levels of insight and responsibility within the wisdom tradition.

Some societies are more freedom-loving than others. It is within these societies that people can live out the full maturity and responsibility of autarchy. If one is born free in these societies, but imagines oneself a slave, the situation is one of lack of self-esteem and lack of trust in one's own abilities. Through the process of Epicurean therapy, individuals would be led to the admittance that a set of false beliefs keeps them from trusting their own abilities and consider strategies to live out their full potential.

One way to expand our comfort zone is to set goals that, in the past, we may have considered unattainable. We may start small and, as we reach our small goals, we may continue on to bigger goals. If they're grounded on reality, then it would be a matter of developing practical strategies to ever attain higher goals, frequently reassessing them and never giving up until they are attained.

One final note here is required in acknowledgement of what I perceive as the need and moral urgency to take care of those who are mentally or physically disabled, or who have special needs in order to reach their full potential. Like many people, I have a loved one who is autistic. This encouraged me to learn about neurodiversity and how people with different brain configurations need an education system and a work environment that tends to their particular needs and exploits their particular talents. When we encourage autistic and special needs people to reach their full potential within their natural limits, we as a society win as much as these individuals do.

The Dangers of Fatal Doctrines

We must enumerate, study and ponder the detrimental effects of false doctrines in human society if we are to establish a firm spiritual foundation for our lives based on true beliefs. This is a crucial matter that deserves an added word of caution.

False doctrines often impose an imagined slavery under the tyranny of the fates, of oracles or of gods whose will is either arbitrary, or difficult to discern. One further insight into the potential dangers of this has to do with how when people embrace divine providence they often derive great comfort from the idea of total surrender to a so-called higher power or to an "other" power. They embrace powerlessness as a false medicine.

While this feels safe and comforting, implicit in the so-called designs of divine providence is the premise that we are not in control, that we have no power. It is prudent to recognize that there are many things over which we have no control. But if refuge-taking becomes castrating, then we may be endangering ourselves.

Refuge-taking can be redemptive if we're still autonomous beings and if we take refuge in true beliefs, or it can serve to consolidate our slavery at the mercy of credulity, wrong views, non-being and of whatever whims arise from the imaginal realm that we associate with the authority that we perceive in divine providence.

People in false belief systems often get attached to their powerlessness. This has been observed by many thinkers in the materialist tradition, prominent among them Marx—who spoke of the opium of the masses--, and Nietzsche—who coined the term "slave religion." Entire systems of values emerge from the paradigm of false belief in Divine Providence that are meant to deny both the freedom and the responsibility of the individual and to expand the projections of our own power not just against divinity but also against the state, the ruling classes, impersonal institutions, or society at large.

The blind belief in "how things have always been" as an ideal breeds automatons and not free and creative men and women. People who trust the decrees of fate, or divine providence, oftentimes allow themselves to degenerate into a state of powerlessness and allow this demoralized state, and the victimization that oftentimes accompanies it, to become part of their very identities. The statistical correlation (Paul, 2005) between poverty and religiosity may be explained by the prevalence of the false doctrine of divine or natural predetermination.

Live Unknown

Epicurus' advice to be apolitical and to live unknown protects our tradition from becoming a tool both of the ruling classes and of the slave mentality. He encouraged his followers, instead, to live in spaces conducive to a life of tranquility and pleasure in the Gardens. Since the spaces of refuge that we create must be subcultures of philosophy, sustainable economics and non-consumerism, the very creation of these spaces inherently constitutes a political and subversive act in our consumerist society.

I have never wished to cater to the crowd; for what I know
they do not approve, and what they approve I do not know.
—Epicurus

Those of us who believe that we vote every day with how we spend our money consider it impossible to be fully apolitical, but we understand the gist of the "Live unknown" maxim. Firstly, one who cares about the opinions of others cannot be said to be autonomous. Secondly, the crown of autarchy is not about control over others, but over ourselves. Autarchy constitutes a micro-political philosophy of individual sovereignty and power that offers unconventional yet satisfying models for living a successful life.

As a spiritual ideal, autarchy requires a deep respect for your own authority and your own decrees. You must have self-discipline and the ability of self-reliance; the setting of goals and later the confidence in your loyalty to yourself and your goals; the trust that you will carry on with Plan B, or Plan C if needed, for the sake of self-sufficiency. If you wish to hold the scepter of autarchy, you must be the general of the army of your senses, mind, willpower, and choices. You must command your habits.

In order to better define and understand philosophical autarchy, it might be useful to imagine in as much detail as possible what the autarch looks like, what the autarch acts like, what he does. He teaches us the art of living by example. The autarch embodies and exemplifies how the autonomous Epicurean philosopher engages productively in the world, how he prospers, how he builds his fortress around his soul and remains always imperturbable, how he effectively administers his inner and outer life. The autarch teaches us great lessons about the dignity that philosophy confers. If you imagine the autarch vividly enough, he might become your personal Life Coach! I will now offer various profiles of autarchy and invite you to create your own profiles.

The Autarchs: Intrepid Epicurean Heroes

An Epicurean must be intrepid. One who cultivates imperturbability, by definition, has a tranquil demeanor, has no trepidations and does not live a life based on fear. But not only does he enjoy mental autonomy: he also has practical matters to attend to. Let's steal the autarch away from his historical realm within the ancient Gardens and place him in our realm, say, as an average American. What is the first thing he does?

Let's name our autarch Hermarchus, after the very first convert to Epicureanism. Sadly, if he really is an average American, he'll be in a lot of debt. He'll want to immediately develop a plan to pay off all debt and either secure a well-paying job or seek multiple streams of income in order to facilitate the fastest road to freedom from debt possible.

As a prudent householder, Hermarchus is not concerned with keeping up with the Joneses—because, as an Epicurean, he knows that worrying about the very unimportant opinions of others is detrimental to happiness—and will likely develop an interest in frugality and simple living. He will use coupons, recycle used items, make the most of what he has, and cut the unnecessary costs from his budget. Cutting unnecessary costs is the easiest way of saving money. This he will continue doing even after paying off his debts, aware that frugality is not just a sign that we are in control of our desires but also the most frequent, reliable slow-and-steady path to wealth and financial independence.

He may accept a roommate in order to save money on rent or mortgage, or live comfortably in a small apartment that meets his needs. His interest in minimalism as a lifestyle leads him to hold a large garage sale and give away or exchange many of the things he no longer uses. He finds that getting rid of clutter has the side of effect of providing clarity of mind.

If he has a plot of land to cultivate in his back yard and if the weather allows, he will grow vegetables, herbs or seasonings there. If he doesn't, but has a small dark room or large enough closet, he may grow mushrooms. He may brew his own beer or other easy-to-make beverages, or perhaps make his own yoghurt. Whatever he enjoys consuming, he will find a way to produce it himself.

He may also exchange some of the surplus from what he produces within a local network of trade in order to support his community's economy because he knows that people prosper through mutual support and cooperation, and he believes very strongly in sustainable economics. He buys local whenever possible. The magnet on his refrigerator says "Small = Beautiful."

Hermarchus heeds Epicurus' advice on frequently associating with pleasant people of like mind and quickly makes close friends with whom he engages in philosophical dis-course frequently. In the process of blending his mind with theirs, sometimes talking about his vulnerabilities and char-acter flaws and listening to theirs, he has quickly become quite close to them and they share similar values. Because of that, and because they are all very skilled at many things, they band together to found a worker cooperative where all workers are owners.

Their business is called "Epicurus Cafe" and not only serves food but also offers an outlet for local writers, poets, musicians, and performers of the spoken word. Because they like creative activities, they use their business space to pro-mote the arts, to host local musicians and poets, and they also celebrate the twentieth of every month with philosophy dis-cussions in their space while enjoying the simple pleasures of sustainably and locally-grown foods.

By having a worker coop, they can be business owners rather than work for someone else. They enjoy job stability and rather than fear being fired, they each look forward to one day selling their share of the business and retiring. They've diminished the risks of being a sole investor by having busi-ness partners who are all equally committed to the same vision and values. They all participate in the business' decision mak-ing processes and they enjoy each other's camaraderie while working.

They also decide to work no more than 30 hours a week each, which allows some of them to pursue other freelance business interests and sources of pleasure on the side. One of the other autarchs is a bartender. Another one owns land and is involved in a local organic farming coop. Another one is a real estate investor. The other two are a couple that owns a hardware business. They all started out in debt, but were dili-gent at living frugally and saving money in order to pay it off and start their business ventures.

Hermarchus does not believe in traditional retirement models: he believes in early, cyclical semi-retirement. In addition to his traditional retirement goals, he has decided to save 20 percent of his income every year so that by the end of every five years, he'll have one year of additional income should he decide to not work, or work on a part-time basis only. Because he does not mind living frugally, he can very easily accomplish his non-traditional retirement goals and is confident that he will have additional time for leisure when he wants it. When he reaches his first cycle of semi-retirement, he feels that he has earned the crown of autarchy.

New Verbiage

Autarch
Early Semi-Retirement Account (ESRA)
Frugality
Minimalism

Task: Create Your Own Autarch Narrative

Each person has unique skills, values, interests, and personality traits that find expression in their work environment. Each person is either in business for himself, or as part of a business must trade skills and time with the business in exchange for a salary. Ergo, each person in our society can, and must, develop his or her own individual business plan. It is up to us to do this, and we may do it consciously and mindfully, or mindlessly (for example, by doing nothing).

Starting with small goals and progressing towards bigger ones, develop your own autarch narrative. What does it mean for YOU to be self-reliant, self-sufficient, and in self-control within your own realm? Within your context and society, how do you make a living? What skills do you trade, and which ones do you wish to develop? How can you maximize the amount and types of wealth you get for those skills?

What additional streams of income or means of production can you acquire? How will you secure enough leisure time for yourself, and perhaps for those you love and with whom you'd like to share your leisure time?

How will you enjoy your leisure time? Who are you? What activities would help you enjoy your independence? What goals and timeline can you set in order to prudently begin to materialize your autarch narrative? What would be the milestones that lead to autarchy?

Task: Assess Your Provision and Retirement Plans

Norman DeWitt (1954) accurately stated that, while like most philosophers we believe that the unanalyzed life is not worth living, we have an added proverb: the unplanned life is not worth living.

Some of our most crucial, life-long tasks have to do with autarchy. They include being confident in our ability to earn a living wage, making retirement and/or early cyclical semi-retirement plans, and making sure to have leisure time to enjoy life with dignity rather than falling in the trap of wage slavery.

Perhaps in addition to our IRA account for traditional retirement, we should also incorporate an ESRA (Early Semi-Retirement Account) into our strategy. In the United States, traditional IRAs allow for substantially equal periodic payments, which may make sense for people close to retirement but not quite there yet. Because tax law changes so often and because so many penalties are tied to early retirement options, please seek advice prior to opting for this. The ability to become self-reliant is available to anyone who sets goals, is persistent, works hard, and finds mentors and associates of like mind to learn from and grow with.

Notice that there is no harm in cooperation among autarchs. The scribes of antiquity all lived together in the Garden, relying on each other as a unit of philosopher friends. Self-reliance and cooperation are not mutually exclusive, in fact, they are both matters of prudence. One person can't do it all.

It is beyond the scope of this book to provide financial or investment advice, but early semi-retirement models oftentimes include the purchase and sale of real estate at the right times and reliance on multiple streams of income. Planning for this helps to provide one with time to enjoy the good things in life without having to wait until the golden years. These matters should all be incorporated into our wisdom traditions.

I am also an advocate of early semi-retirement cycles for an additional, pragmatic reason: it serves as a rehearsal for the real thing, and this is far more important than most people think. We must know how we wish to retire so we can plan for it and enjoy it. If we build our entire identity and social life around our job and don't know what we'll do when we retire, like many unsuccessful retirees we will be depressed when we find ourselves without it. We will feel unproductive and useless rather than experience retirement as a time to reap the fruits of our labor.

We have to build an identity of leisure, an identity outside of our jobs: learn our likes, our hobbies, our passions, get better at doing the things that we are passionate about, and perhaps even learn to make money on the side while doing them. If we find pleasure in our streams of income, then leisure and productivity are one and the same.

Semi-retirement is a chance to be productive by earning a part-time wage doing what we love as part of our retirement. In other words, just as we should reinvent labor, so should we reinvent retirement.

References

DeWitt, Norman. *Epicurus and His Philosophy.* (University of Minnesota Press, 1954).

Kelso, Louis and Adler, Mortimer. *The Capitalist Manifesto* (New York: Random House, 1958).

Kelso, Louis and Hetter, Patricia. *Two-Factor Theory* (New York: Vintage Press, 1968).

Paul, Gregory. "Cross-National Correlations of Quantifiable Societal Health with Popular Religiosity and Secularism in the Prosperous Democracies." *Journal of Religion & Society*, Volume 7 (2005). Retrieved from http://moses.creighton.edu/jrs/2005/2005-11.pdf

X

HOLY VERSUS WHOLESOME: THE CASE FOR SECULAR ETHICS

Epicurus teaches that justice is a social and cultural construct based on our societal agreements. As such, we are as a society called to assume full responsibility for the systems of justice that we establish and the ethical doctrines that we teach.

Sometimes good ethical concepts derive from the wrong foundations and/or lead to the wrong conclusions because they are tied to supernatural claims that generate confusion: an anti-abortion Christian who does not have a solid foundation in the ethical principles of non-violence might approve of war or remain uncritical of the cruelty of the meat industry, all while being ostentatious about her pro-life stance. This is a symptom of an incoherent worldview.

If someone really practices a non-violent lifestyle, is anti-war and anti-abortion, *and* boycotts the meat industry and other industries based on cruelty, then *that* seems coherent and deserves the pro-life label. The question I raise here is one of consistency and coherence of one's worldview, not the merit of a label.

Inconsistency is not our only critique of non-naturalist ethics. There are instances where religious ethics are outright dangerous and evil. We know of honor killings of young women by their Muslim fathers or brothers, of a "Kill the Gays" bill in Uganda, and the Old Testament (not to mention history) teems with violent episodes of genocide and "holy" war (if a war can be deemed holy). The Levite Code in the Bible supports slavery, the stoning to death of one's sons for drinking alcohol, and the sale of women. The Hindu epic of Ramayana legitimizes widow suicide.

A Healthy Mind in a Healthy Body. —Latin Adage

When asked, "Whence do you derive your values?", many people refer back to their religious upbringing, but few have done the intellectual work of analyzing with a healthy level of rigor the foundations of those teachings. On the other hand, it is impossible to find fault in the secular ideal *Mens sana in corpore sano*. What could possibly be wrong with a healthy mind in a healthy body?

The Latin word *sano*, which translates as sane or healthy in English, shares semantic roots with the words saintly and sanctity. Somewhere in history, the two notions became separate ideals in the same way that holy and wholesome are separate ideas today in the English language. By confusing ethics with religion, society has made a significant shift away from healthy ethics and common sense and put aside natural philosophy in favor of supernatural credulity. To be good is then to believe, not necessarily to be sane or healthy. Society suffers as a result.

The notion of that which is holy inherits baggage that remains with us to this day: it was tied to taboos, to irrational fears, and to fundamental negations of life, not all of which were wholesome.

That Which Is Set Apart

The saintly, the holy, the sacred, the Biblical notion of "kedosh," is tied to that which is set apart, that which is dedicated (to a deity or to a cause). When a thing is sacrificed (*sacri-ficare*), it is by definition made sacred. It cannot be used for trivial purposes. It's imbued with a special dignity and, religious people believe, with a sort of supernatural power.

The holy also has the sense of being secret, that which cannot be touched or spoken of. The Bible forbids the uttering of the name of its god. Women who are menstruating are unclean and must live separately. There are things that are taboo, forbidden, because they are holy: working on the sabbath, offering an unclean animal to a god, and even eating shrimp, pork and other arbitrary categories of food. While these notions help to preserve some sort of social order, they carry with them mental slavery and unnecessary restrictions that have nothing to do with true ethical questions and which, by virtue of being set apart, claim to be above reproach. The holy is not always the wholesome.

The sacrifice of an animal, from the perspective of non-violent ideals, is considered unethical and unwholesome, yet it is a holy event. The stoning of someone for working on a sabbath is also unwholesome, yet according to the Old Testament this was the holy duty of those who lived under Moses' rule. There is, therefore, a fundamental distinction between living a holy life and living a wholesome life although many would have us believe that a holy life is by definition wholesome.

The inability to question authority and tradition, implicit in the sense of the holy as that which is secret and cannot be touched or spoken of, carries additional baggage: we are not encouraged to raise legitimate questions about abuses or illegitimate authority. The abuse of thousands of children by Catholic priests, which has taken place over generations, reveals a culture of depredation that could have only developed within the context of a submissive, unquestioning flock.

It is absolutely moral and necessary to demand transparency of our leaders, religious or secular. Only tyranny is served when we don't and it is often tyrants who require our child-like unquestioning obedience.

Censorship must be addressed as a particularly detestable example of latent and overt tendencies towards religious totalitarianism. Book-burning hysterias and a general culture of hostility against wisdom are, in part, what led to the closing of Epicurean schools, the destruction of Epicurus' over 300 scrolls, and the very efficient defamation campaign against philosophical hedonists throughout the centuries. Even today, many religious groups use the word "hedonist" as an insult and almost no one frames serious private and public ethical questions within the proper discourse of hedonic calculus, which is where they belong. It's easy to forget the cultural wealth that we've lost because we will never truly know how much we've lost as a result of religious censorship. All we can say is that we will forever be an intellectually poorer species than we could have been.

No one can argue that all taboos are unwholesome, and in fact many would argue—rightly, in my opinion—that children are easily influenced by their authority figures and that the notion of taboo is needed if we are to rear wholesome children: there are limits to set. But only taboos that are wholesome and not based on irrational fear should be encouraged.

While people of all religions do oftentimes great and wholesome things inspired by their belief, they also engage in amoral and immoral behavior for the sake of the same belief. A sane, sophisticated system of ethics must, at the very least, differentiate clearly between the holy and the wholesome and name religious taboos that are amoral or unwholesome as such.

Hygiene and Health

Many holy practices have their origin in hygiene as a means to prevent disease. They are sane and have to do with health. The holy baths taken by Jews, Muslims, Hindus and other groups, are an example of such practices.

Similarly, Native Americans translate spiritual power as medicine and, like many ancient cultures, tie their folklore to ancient healing practices, some of which are legitimate. Many pharmaceutical companies have made their fortunes by researching and patenting the herbal and natural wisdom of traditional healers. For instance, the relaxing properties of hops or linden and the invigorating effects of maca were first discovered by ancestors who sought their medicine in nature.

Cleanliness and other healthy practices are, then, a matter of ethics and a necessity for the good life since they prevent disease and unnecessary pain. The removal of harmful germs within the household, daily bodily hygiene, and a healthy diet are all important ethical concerns.

It is sometimes difficult to scientifically assess the damage done by unwholesome thoughts, violent or morbid imagery in films or in games, chaotic music, or the association of foul-mouthed friends with a bad character. But if the prevalence of post-traumatic stress disorder among those commissioned to kill in other countries is any indication, it seems that what we feed our minds becomes our reality and remains with us long after we experience it.

Only through mindfulness and introspection can we notice the anxiety caused by certain music and the serenity caused by other music, the demeaning influence of bad friends and the good influence of others, or the anxious impulses generated by violent or morbid films and scenes, not to mention abusive relations. Mental hygiene is, therefore, just as important as bodily hygiene.

Many of the ways in which Epicurean philosophy enriches our lives have to do with mental sanity and health and they are discussed elsewhere in this book. Bodily health is also important, and since there is no boundary between mind and body, both mental and bodily hygiene should be cultivated. Without vibrant health, it can be difficult to live a pleasant life.

Natural Justice

Some of the enemies of Epicurus (well, the usual suspects ... the Platonists) argued that, because the Canon (which will be discussed later in detail) makes each person able to discern truth independently using criteria as subjective as the pain-pleasure principle, therefore Epicureans were not capable of carrying out the duties and responsibilities of a good citizen. These types of arguments were founded in Platonic notions of justice that attributed supernatural or metaphysical qualities to justice and made it necessary for Epicurus to articulate a non-metaphysical teaching which later became fundamental to our system of laws: the social contract.

While religious traditions propose rudimentary systems of so-called justice, such as the Islamic shari'a where women's testimony is worth half that of men's and where any criticism of religion is punishable by death, Epicurus proposes a theory of justice founded on the social contract.

Natural justice is a pledge of reciprocal benefit, to prevent
one man from harming or being harmed by another ...
It is impossible for a man who secretly violates the terms
of the agreement not to harm or be harmed to feel confident
that he will remain undiscovered, even if he has already
escaped ten thousand times; for until his death he is never
sure that he will not be detected.
—Principal Doctrines 31, 35

In other words, rather than justice emerging from abstract and un-organic principles, from arbitrary authority or from gods, Epicurus said that living agents enter into contracts naturally. What this contractarian theory of justice means, in practice, is that we created and enacted our laws and we, of course, may also change them.

Many opponents of Epicurus have argued that, following his train of thought, an Epicurean would commit theft or other crimes if he knew he was going to get away with it. What Epicurus teaches in (above-cited) PD 35, however, is that both Epicureans and non-Epicureans are likely to live with guilt and shame if they fail to uphold the social agreement not to harm another. Failure to uphold one's side of the bargain produces shame, guilt, fines, politically and socially-upheld penalties and other mechanisms which help conserve the social order.

Some Final Considerations

It is unfair to be virulently critical of religious practices that are neither harmful nor unwholesome, for they harm no one except for being, perhaps, a waste of time, an unnecessary restriction, or merely an inconvenience. Many of these practices (like the singing of religious songs) add a considerable amount of aesthetic value and beauty to the lives of people. If they are a source of beauty and pleasure for practitioners, then they are by definition good. Like many other instances where we are not sure whether an act is good or bad, hedonic calculus can help to make a determination in these cases.

In the case of unwholesome practices that generate unnecessary pain (circumcision, homophobia, animal sacrifice), some of us feel that it is our duty to point out the instances where religion is positively immoral. Having said that, there is no doubt that a religious person can be perfectly ethical, particularly if that person has a disposition for good judgment.

A secular approach to ethics, a focus on sanity instead of sanctity, on the wholesome and healthy instead of the holy as an ethical ideal, does much to help liberate humans from superstition and groundless fear. These secular ethical notions do not carry the baggage of religious ones and are generally easy to recognize, teach, and put into practice.

Secular ethical philosophers should therefore get used to speaking of sanity, of healthy lifestyles, of wholesome ideals and friends, and so on, and should throughout their lifetimes develop their own wisdom traditions around what these things—and their opposites—mean in practice.

New Verbiage

Natural Justice
The Social Contract

XI

THE CANON: THE STANDARD OF TRUTH

The body of knowledge within Epicurean philosophy is organized into the Canon, Physics, and Ethics. The Canon explains Epicurean epistemology: our theory of knowledge and the legitimate ways to acquire it. Physics deals with atomism and the description of ultimate reality. Ethics deals with the science of determining the proper way to make choices and live the good life. Most of this book deals with ethics, which is where we find most of the practical applications of Epicureanism.

How is legitimate wisdom acquired? That is the concern of the Canon, which translates as "rule" or "measuring stick" and sets the foundation for our ability to grasp reality as it really is and is so important to us that some Epicureans think of it as the very first thing that every Epicurean must have a clear understanding of.

The Canon is the title of the scroll that Epicurus wrote explaining his theory of knowledge, the original of which is lost to us. It's also known as the book that fell from heaven—derisively by opponents and reverently or perhaps humorously among adherents, since they were known to promote good humor. It would be unfair to treat the subject of the value of a wisdom tradition without first delving into the basics of the Canon, which sets the rules for establishing truth.

Epicurus proposed that, as information gatherers, we are born with a tool kit that includes three criteria—the canon's tripod, the three legs on which it stands—to discern reality: sensations (the information we derive from the five senses—hearing, touch, smell, vision and taste), anticipations (innate pre-conceptions), and feelings (the pain/pleasure principle).

Our discussion of the Canon must be prefaced by explaining that knowledge, like desires, may be classified into necessary or unnecessary, as well as into natural or unnatural, with natural and necessary knowledge assuming a position of priority. We only need to know what's necessary for our peace and safety. Knowledge beyond this may be interesting, and it may even be a source of pleasure, but it's unnecessary. Nature sets limits within which we gain knowledge, and our faculties allow us to easily gain the knowledge that is natural and necessary.

Data fed to us from the senses is necessary to verify spurious claims, supernatural or otherwise. If claims seem difficult to believe, we should reserve judgment until the senses have verified them. It is generally possible to subject claims to experiments and observation and to corroborate them through the five senses, or perhaps utilizing telescopes, microscopes, and other scientific devices that enhance the reach of our senses.

This is perhaps most important when we have a strong desire to believe something for which there is no supporting evidence: a true philosopher must able to discern clearly between "I believe ..." and "I would like to think ..."

The criterion of the aversion/pleasure mechanism further roots our epistemology in nature as our guide. We must be able to derive necessary and natural knowledge from the environment in which we operate. Sometimes this information is vital to our survival, safety, health and happiness. When knowledge is unnecessary our feelings are generally indifferent toward it, but generally poison is bitter and juices high in nutrition are sweet. Friends are pleasant and enemies are unpleasant, and so on. It is understood that we react to these things because they matter to our well-being.

Nature guides different creatures by different means. Most mammals smell their food prior to eating it: generally, if it smells repugnant (to them), it's bad (for them). It carries germs and toxins that are to be avoided. But then vultures and other carnivorous animals who have in their guts the powerful enzymes needed to consume rotting meat, find pleasure in the smell of it. Nature guides them. Both the senses (smell) and the feelings (aversion or pleasure) are needed in order to determine whether a food is edible, and this information varies by species. Under normal conditions, we are able to determine the good by our senses and by the pain/pleasure principle.

The Canon is unique among early epistemological theories in that it is deeply rooted in biology and in the theory of natural selection. Carnivorous animals that did not find pleasure in meat would have been unable to survive and pass on their genes, whereas their counterparts who allowed themselves to be led by pleasure successfully developed hunting strategies—some of which required elaborate social skills—survived and passed on their genes. Over many generations, those that adapted best continued to pass on their genes and specialize in their survival strategies.

At times, auspicious collaborations emerge between more than one species. The wolf became man's hunting and herding companion and the two species find so much pleasure in each other that the dog is considered man's best friend. Human fishermen in Brazil have learned to communicate with dolphins effectively enough to fish together (Welsh, 2012). Plants use bees to disperse their seeds, and bees find pleasure in their pollen.

These natural covenants of mutual benefit among species can sometimes become so crucial to their survival that they become embedded in their very personalities. Many humans find their pets irresistibly adorable because domestic dogs and cats possess many of the same attributes as human babies as a result of speciation and interaction with humans. We have learned to access each other's evolutionary triggers. The human has become the alpha in the pack and the dog, another family member.

These natural covenants are, as far as I understand them, distinct from Epicurus' concept of natural justice. They are what may happen when our anticipations (inherited psychological traits) are triggered by another species. Natural justice emerges, not from instinct, but from free agency. It is here that we must address the third leg of the Canon's tripod: anticipations.

Just as we inherit physical traits from our ancestors, we also inherit psychological traits, instincts or faculties. If a babe did not anticipate a nipple, it would not suckle. Also, couples would not bond and mate, and people would not recognize each other as social entities, or their food sources. Human face recognition is one of the first things that a child is pre-programmed for.

Plants and animals would not be able to attune themselves biologically to the circadian rhythms: recent studies show that plants carry out simple, chemical mathematics in order to determine how much starch to consume to last until dawn (Scialdone et al., 2013). All of these innate faculties are part of what we know as anticipations.

One important thing to note about anticipations is that they are inherited instincts. In other words, they are innate and biological. They exist prior to reason and the formation of memories and cognitive processes and are pre-rational, although—to be fair—we must recognize that proponents of epigenetics and some Epicurean thinkers believe that memories can trigger strong enough impulses to become transferable within only one generation.

The three legs of Epicurus' tripod of truth (senses, anticipations and feelings) are rooted in our biological, material reality. Unlike false, yet popular, speculative philosophies, Epicureanism offers a naturalistic, scientific epistemology which has a firm foundation in biology and in observable reality.

Other traditions, like Objectivism and its predecessor Aristotelianism, opulently praise logic and reason to the detriment of the pain/pleasure faculty, and thus become divorced from nature and from the tangibles of ethics. Objectivism is therefore not fit to address serious moral problems of our day like the corporate attempts to privatize water which generated the Bolivian Water Wars or the prevalence of corruption in the financial industry which caused the loss of over 40 percent of Americans' retirement savings in 2008. When we generate this much unnecessary suffering in the name of ideals, our ethics have become unwholesome.

Reason can only work with the data that we get from our perceiving organs and, while it is of great importance as a tool for approaching reality, it is not part of the tripod of truth. For example, we can only infer that reality is made up of atoms and the void after we have observed directly that there is movement, and that matter therefore must constantly find space to move into. We can only infer that a sentient being exists if we observe it: non-physical beings are, by definition, non-existent and do not require sacrifices or food. A house cat or dog, however, will visibly and tangibly starve and suffer if not fed.

Without the initial sense perception, reason has no raw material from which to draw conclusions. And reason can, and often does, draw the wrong conclusions just as a calculator would, if fed the wrong data or if working from the wrong premises, or if it does away completely from sense data or from the pleasure/pain mechanism. Therefore, reason is not part of our tripod. The faculties that are included in the Canon give us raw, unprocessed, pre-rational data without which reason is useless in our immediate apprehension of reality.

This is not to say that reason is unimportant, but we believe that it is overrated and only useful as a secondary tool within the checks and balances that the Canon establishes. Unlike the three sets of faculties that are included in the Canon, which deal in tangibles, reason can only serve to calculate and to infer and can sometimes divorce us from tangible reality.

We must also keep in mind that, to the Platonists, reason was a separate entity, a deity with a concrete identity. We hold this to be a false view. There is absolutely no reason to believe that our reasoning faculty is divine or exists in a supernatural or eternal realm, however this view was common during the days of Epicurus.

Without the reference points of pleasure and pain, people invent imaginary and abstract standards for ethics that are divorced from reality and generate vast amounts of unnecessary suffering. It is impossible to accurately carry out hedonic calculus based on these false beliefs. A terrorist campaign may be deemed holy, in spite of how much more pain than pleasure it causes. Atheists are executed for apostasy in some countries and women stoned for adultery, leaving their children orphaned. An abortion may be deemed immoral even if it prevents the death of the mother. People in happy gay relationships are demoralized and shunned by their own families.

Invariably these errors in hedonic calculus are carried out because the tangibles of ethics have been ignored, which results in a distortion of people's moral compass. Pleasure is the only *real* ethical guide. It returns our conversations about ethics to the natural context where these conversations belong: the well-being of sentient beings.

Ethics exists for the sake of life and must be compassionately woven into the concerns of the living. Without pleasure, and nature, as our guide we fail to understand what really matters, we fail to accurately identify those things that make life worth living. We lose our compassion and build fictional, baseless ethical standards when we forget that ethics only exists for the sake of sentient beings, that it is only because of pain and pleasure that there is a need and an imperative for the existence of ethics.

Our philosophical tradition is the only one that offers a fully cogent, scientific approach to ethics. It is of great importance to understand that our inherent morals, the morals taught by nature itself, are found within the Canon, which is our connection to reality.

In other words, the reason why justice and friendship are good is because they are pleasant and the reason why injustice, violence, enmity and hatred are bad is because they feel painful. These are the tangibles of ethics.

References

Scialdone, A. *et al.* (2013). "Arabidopsis plants perform arithmetic division to prevent starvation at night." *eLife,* June 25, 2013. http://elife.elifesciences.org/content/2/e00669

Welsh, Jennifer. "Dolphins Help Fishermen Catch Fish." *LiveScience.com,* May 1, 2012. Retrieved from http://www.livescience.com/20027-dolphins-work-fishermen.html

XII

PHYSICS: THE NATURE OF THINGS

While doing research for this book, I informally subjected the twelve principles of Epicurus' physics to feedback from various sources more or less familiar with physics in order to get a sense of how relevant they still are when compared to modern scientific understanding. There did not exist complete agreement between respondents on all principles, and some of the divergences of opinion had to do with the meanings attached to words.

I noticed among some of the respondents (some of whom had supernatural beliefs) a considerable amount of speculation around quantum physics which, if we are to judge by films like *What the Bleep Do We Know*, introduce a high level of metaphysics and Platonic whim which raises credibility questions. In that film, New Age gurus use quantum verbiage to propose all kinds of metaphysical hypotheses without fully understanding the complex world of quantum physics, of which scientist Richard Feynman has been quoted, most famously by Richard Dawkins, as saying "If you think you understand quantum theory, then you don't understand quantum theory."

Be mindful that some of the replies make reference to quantum physics or may have otherwise come from people with a more or less limited understanding of physics. The first two of the twelve principles are:

Matter is uncreatable.

Matter is indestructible.

When we take matter as being the same thing as energy, the principles are generally held to still be true. However, if we take matter to refer to particles, then these are creatable and destructible. What is indestructible is energy, which all matter translates into.

For a more complete understanding of how energy translates into matter, we must learn Einstein's relativity equation: $E=mc^2$, where E stands for energy, m stands for mass and c stands for the speed of light. The equation means that energy is equal to matter multiplied by the speed of light squared.

It is beyond the scope of this book to define energy in detail, but with regards to the first two principles, we must remind ourselves of the reasoning behind these principles and of Epicurus' argument against the Platonists and creationists that nothing comes from nothing. This, we believe, is the essence of the first two principles and the reason why they matter in our cosmology. The third principle states:

The universe consists of solid bodies and void.

Part of the controversy of this statement deals with semantics: the void is not a thing, it's nothing. Ergo, it cannot be said to exist. However, atomic particles require space and context, they require a realm of possibility and opportunity, so in some way space must be part of reality. Otherwise, all space would be filled instead of empty and all movement would be impossible. Because movement exists, we must infer that the void exists among the particles and this is how atoms and the void became the binary language of reality in the atomist tradition.

Again, we must always keep in mind that these principles arise as a reaction to confusing and fraudulent Platonist views of reality. What this principle is meant to deny is the existence of a supernatural, unnatural or non-material realm. All real things exist within nature. Things that aren't material, are merely imaginary and do not exist in reality. Ancient atomists taught that all reality must be anchored in matter. The fourth principle states:

Solid bodies are either compounds or simple.

The ancient atomists were the first ones to propose the existence of the atom, but their atomic theory was very different from the modern one. Science later adopted the word *atomoi*, which originates in the Greek meaning "that which cannot be divided." Since atoms are made up of electrons, protons and neutrons, it seems like this principle may be true or false depending on the definition of its terms.

Cassius Amicus, of the newepicurean.com webpage, at one point proposed that instead of atoms the term particles should be used today in any discussion of the twelve principles in order to avoid confusion, but ultimately he believes that whatever word we use is fine as long as it is defined as being undividable.

Having said all that, it's true that atoms bind together to form molecules and elements, and so on in increasing complexity, so that this principle is upheld by the modern Epicurean school. The fifth and sixth principles state:

The multitude of atoms is infinite.

The void is infinite in extent.

This is today generally thought to have no supporting evidence, or to remain unverifiable, due to observational horizons. However, as far as we can observe, the universe seems to expand in all directions without pushing against a visible boundary. The seventh principle states:

The atoms are always in motion.

This is today held to be true, and the rate of its motion is called temperature. The eighth principle states:

The speed of atomic motion is uniform.

The uniformity of speed of atomic motion is in question, although not everyone understands what is meant by this uniformity. Different atoms have different rates of vibration. The ninth principle states:

Motion is linear in space, vibratory in compounds.

The linearity of motion can be thought of as part of Newton's first law of motion (inertia) which states that things in motion have a tendency to continue said motion whereas static things have a tendency to remain static. The meaning of the word linear, of course, must be relative to gravity. More than one source of gravity would blur the linearity of movement.

The vibration of compounds is tied to Brownian Motion, which deals with the observation by Robert Brown during the nineteenth century of random movement of particles in water and his later theorizing that this movement was caused by the vibration of molecules. The tenth principle states:

Atoms are capable of swerving slightly at any point in space or time.

Depending on whom we ask, and how the swerve is defined, we may get the broad answer that atoms (or particles) do exhibit motion, or that the swerve theory is now discredited. The ancient idea of the swerve involved chaotic motion. It was believed that atoms exhibited from time to time a quality of random movement in the same manner that we know today genes, periodically, also exhibit random mutations every so many generations which can be traced back in time.

Non-determinism and non-fatalism is the reasoning behind the swerve. In other words, if particles exhibited steady and eternally predictable movement, all things would have been pre-determined.

Early atomists (including Epicurus' teacher, Nausiphanes) believed that atoms were originally perpetually falling into the void in one direction. Our current understanding of gravity and its effects on particles makes the swerve physically unnecessary, but it remains philosophically necessary and relevant. The swerve is, to us, a symbol of whatever freedom human and animal agents exhibit in nature.

According to Pierre-Marie Morel (2009), although the swerve does not explain how volition happens, it invites us to consider "a break in the necessary mechanical chain of physical causation." The swerve, in our tradition, serves to ignite a philosophical theory of freedom because it seeks to explain random change, and therefore life and volition in sentient beings. It explains why we're not automatons and why things are not predetermined in the universe.

The important thing to know about the modern version of the doctrine of the swerve and what our tradition has to say about it is that the motion of atoms, and of heavenly bodies for that matter, is not controlled by gods or by providence, and that therefore random motion is a necessary part of a non-deterministic cosmos. Whatever laws govern our cosmos are natural, not supernatural. Although the original scientific explanation was flawed, the underlying reasoning is still relevant, it still informs the modern scientific worldview and is of huge importance. The eleventh principle states:

**Atoms are characterized by three qualities:
weight, shape and size.**

Since weight is a function of mass acted on by gravity, perhaps mass would be the inherent property whereas weight is more accurately described as the result of whatever gravity affects the particle.

Otherwise, the list of atomic qualities is accurate but, depending on whom one asks, it lacks other attributes such as inertia, gravitation (again, relative to other objects), spin, density (mass divided by volume), and volume or size. Some say shape and size are meaningless at these scales. Others say the word "pattern" may be more accurate than "shape."

The limited number of qualities attributed to particles might be explained by the fact that Epicurus spoke of incidental (symptomatic) and non-incidental (*symbebekotic*, or those that would fundamentally change an object) properties of particles. Non-incidental qualities are essential and necessary to the identity of a molecule or body. On the other hand, if symptomatic properties change, the particle would still remain what it is. Symptomatic properties are, therefore, secondary and non-essential. The twelfth and final principle states:

The number of the different shapes is not infinite, merely innumerable.

This principle has generated controversy and confusion due to its general lack of clarity when translated into modern physics. The meaning of this appears to be that there is a limited number of combinations of atoms, perhaps of elements. Hence, the doctrine of innumerable worlds, which is based on the idea that if you go far enough in all directions, you will begin to see the eternal repetition of similar combinations of atoms, including planetary systems like our own.

Just as in his poem *De Rerum Natura*, Lucretius proposed various proto-scientific and scientific theories to give potential naturalist explanations for phenomena such as lightning and the movement of celestial bodies that had been previously attributed to supernatural beings, Epicurus did the same in his physics. Many of Epicurus' and Lucretius' explanations were later found to be flawed or incomplete, but all the credible alternative views that ultimately came to be accepted invariably provided natural explanations and placed us firmly within the context of a natural cosmology.

As for Epicurus' reasoning behind the twelve principles, we should bear in mind that the gist of them has to do, in part, with there being eternally reliable principles in nature that can be scientifically discerned, that reality is firm and material, and that no supernatural claims need to be made about natural phenomena. We are naturalist philosophers. Nature and reality are one and the same.

References

Lucretius Carus, Titus. *De Rerum Natura*. Leonard, William E. (Trans.). Retrieved from http://classics.mit.edu/Carus/nature_things.html

Morel, Pierre-Marie. "Epicurean Atomism," in Warren, James (Ed.), *The Cambridge Companion to Epicureanism* (New York: Cambridge University Press, 2009).

XIII

ON THE MATTER OF CULTURAL CONTINUITY

The Epicurean Oath and the Plural Leadership Models

One of the stated goals of the Society of Friends of Epicurus is to ensure the cultural continuity of the tradition. There are several possible ways of implementing a system that internally facilitates said continuity. I will first discuss the oath, and then the plural leadership model.

What constitutes conversion? What defines an Epicurean practitioner, as opposed to merely someone who admires Epicurus or who considers our tradition an intellectual curiosity without adhering to it? According to the Iberian philosopher Seneca, Epicurus instituted a hierarchical and initiatory system of levels among his followers and had them swear an oath on his core tenets. Through that oath, a person became a follower of Epicurus and expressed his resolve to follow the teachings.

The oath can additionally serve to establish the premise for therapy. A pupil must express the resolution to be happy and tranquil, the resolution to cultivate imperturbability and to apply Epicurean teachings and methodology as a pre-requisite for therapy. Otherwise, the work of therapy would be possibly as inappropriate as a Catholic expecting a Buddhist to undergo the sacrament of confession. By formally declaring the oath, the pupil properly enters into an agreement which creates the dynamic necessary for the process of applied philosophy, including the expectations from other Epicureans.

The oath, however, should not be actively encouraged and there shouldn't be a recruitment process in the conventional sense. People should thoroughly evaluate the worth and usefulness of Epicurean teachings prior to any commitment. If a person (who may or may not take on the teaching mission) agrees with the general teaching, applies it within his process of pursuit of happiness, and seeks the association of others of like mind—because identity is a social construct—then said person should be considered an Epicurean.

Philodemus offered us the following confessional oath: "I will be faithful to Epicurus according to whom it has been my choice to live." Notice that Philodemus' oath accentuates the idea of our choice. Some people may be reluctant to affirm an oath to a historical person, preferring instead to affirm an oath to his ideas. Adapted accordingly, the oath would be: "I will be faithful to Epicureanism according to which it has been my choice to live."

The oath may act as a remedy for people who lack resolve. It builds stronger resolution and has therapeutic value. As with some experiences of religious conversion for people going through difficulties, healing and transformation of the character can be initiated through the oath and it may have therapeutic benefits.

While the oath may be useful in the process of ensuring our tradition's continuity and realizing its therapeutic value, the initiatory system and hierarchy that existed in antiquity (as related by Norman DeWitt in his *Organization and Procedure in Epicurean Groups*) is not practical or necessary in our day and age. Instead, a modern approach to methods of passing down the tradition should develop and evolve organically.

One alternative way to ensure the cultural continuity and the transferal of our wisdom tradition would be to instate four Epicurean Guides in every Garden whose opinions are highly regarded because they are the most knowledgeable members of the community, as the modern Gardens in Greece have done. These Gardens are not physical spaces with plants, but rather communities of philosopher-friends who practice Epicureanism within a certain geographical proximity.

I suspect this tradition of having four Guides per Garden was done in commemoration of "the Men," the four original founding fathers of Epicureanism (Epicurus, Metrodorus, Hermarchus, and Polyaenus). Under this model, if the community loses one leader, the other Guides can step in. As a four-headed creature, the collective effort would not dissipate, but would simply reorganize. If this model is implemented faithfully and without interruption, even if only in a few cities, Epicurean tradition could continue to be viable, in theory, for the rest of history.

I do not think that the oath method and the plural leadership method are mutually exclusive. I believe they can strengthen each other and produce various models of interaction and learning. Taking the time to implement formal processes of teaching and learning Epicureanism can serve to formally recognize in Epicurean philosophy the same level of worth and of dignity that Epicureanism confers upon humanity. The implementation of its continuity is a sign of respect for the tradition.

Learning from Other Wisdom Traditions

Let's look at how other contemporary wisdom traditions succeed at preserving themselves and evaluate the merits and potential usefulness of their methods.

In the South American nations of Bolivia and Ecuador, the constitution is partly inspired by the aboriginal, First Nations wisdom tradition known as *sumak kawsay*, which translates as "the good life," or "good living." This philosophical concept is defined in detail in the constitution as involving better and more sustainable human relations in harmony with nature, less consumerism, taking only what is necessary in order to satisfy one's desires, being able to love and be loved, having time for leisure and contemplation, protection of liberty, and healthy flourishing of all in harmony with nature.

For example the constitution of Ecuador includes the following provisions:

Article 22. Persons have the right to develop their creative capacity, to the commendable and steady exercise of cultural and artistic activities, and to benefit from the protection of moral and heritage rights that pertain to them as a result of the scientific, literary or artistic productions of which they are the authors. ...

Article 24. Persons have the right to recreation and leisure, the practice of sports and free time.

Article 25. Persons have the right to enjoy the benefits and applications of scientific progress and ancestral wisdom.

It's as if Epicurus had been one of their great ancestral sages! The ability to live according to this noble code of ethics is guaranteed by the law of the land.

Thomas Jefferson, a self-proclaimed Epicurean who owned five copies of *De Rerum Natura*, enshrined in our Declaration of Independence the right to the pursuit of happiness and other principles which bear the fingerprints of Epicurus. However, the apolitical nature of Epicureanism means that political or legislative influence is not the way in which it will, or should, preserve itself. Philosophical insight cannot be imposed from the top down.

What we *can* learn from the South American model for preserving the aboriginal wisdom tradition is that this consciousness of "good living" started at the grassroots level in populations that have historically enjoyed a strong communitarian spirit. As a result of the soundness and robustness of this philosophy, it became a source of popular pride. In other words, it gained legitimacy by becoming a philosophy of the people.

Ancient Scandinavians had bards known as the *skalds* who, through poetry, performance and music, kept their ancestral wisdom alive. If many of the verses of the *Havamál* sound like nuggets of wisdom given by an elder to a younger person in a family, it's thanks to the *skalds'* ability to preserve the lore of their ancestors, and to later compile it in writing after centuries of oral tradition. Lucretius also used poetry effectively to impart the teachings.

What we can learn from the *skalds* is that respect for the elders and those who are more knowledgeable, and a habit of listening profitably to them and passing on their lore, produces a sense of pride and of inter-generational transcendence. Modern forms of cultural expressions and of media should be applied to promote and preserve the Epicurean wisdom of those that came before and grassroots wisdom traditions should be nurtured.

Wisdom traditions can also take the form of plays or myths that are retold yearly at festivals. The Hindu epic of the *Ramayana* has been used for centuries to teach people how to properly and compassionately treat each other. It exemplifies the ideal roles of husband and wife, of loving friends, of caring masters and dutiful servants, etc. in a manner which teaches human values. Unfortunately, the Ramayana has also been used by the ruling classes to perpetuate gender and class roles that are detrimental to the flourishing of women and members of various groups.

The Ramayana contains many valuable life lessons and pearls of wisdom such as "a word is like an arrow: once spoken, it cannot be taken back," and dramatizes what happens when people run after vain desires.

Another effect of the constant retelling of the story is that it has accumulated additions and commentaries by the gurus over the course of the generations so that it's become a valuable, vibrant, living and evolving compendium of folklore. The development of a cultural cycle of philosophy festivals where the life and memory of Epicurus are narrated and celebrated might help to not just popularize our wisdom tradition, but also to allow it to adapt and grow with a life of its own.

We must not ignore the Judeo-Christian and Islamic tradition of preserving wisdom in the form of revered scripture, which has perpetuated cultural memes for millennia and has already crossed over into humanism by inspiring A.C. Grayling's *The Good Book*, which imitates the editorial style and spirit of the Bible and Quran, but is entirely secular.

There are numerous moving Biblical adages that resonate deeply with human experience. "Pride comes before the fall" reminds us to not be too arrogant. The final chapter of Proverbs lists the qualities of a resourceful and entrepreneurial woman (or man, for that matter). There are historical moments that have been dramatically marked by passages from scripture. Martin Luther King's reference to the Book of Amos during his legendary civil rights speech is still profoundly moving and is forever etched into America's collective memory. After repudiating the animal sacrifices and displays of piety unaccompanied by social justice, the text concludes:

> *But let justice roll down like waters, and righteousness like an ever-flowing stream.*
>
> —Amos 5:24

Epicureans have our own scriptural tradition. We have the Vatican Sayings, the Principal Doctrines, several letters by our founder, Lucretius' poem *On the Nature of Things*, whatever remains of the contents of Diogenes' Wall, and a few other collections of adages gathered for didactic purposes by our predecessors.

We also have *The Jefferson Bible*, a naturalist approach that honors the teachings of Jesus of Nazareth, and a twenty-first century version of it issued by the American Humanist Association which celebrates the wisdom of the Quran, Bhagavad Gita and other texts.

Another example of wisdom traditions that successfully self-preserve can be seen in the martial arts, where lore is passed down from the masters to the students via a system of initiations and a curriculum of instruction where cords, ribbons or other symbols are given at every grade. In some traditions—like capoeira—the initiate also receives a new name at the beginning of his training, which strengthens his *capoeirista* identity.

Naming traditions have an interesting history among the laughing philosophers, those that (like the Epicureans) did not cater to the *polis* and to traditional authority. We know from ancient sources that Epicurus used to give endearing names to many of his associates, and that he mocked his teacher Nausiphanes by calling him the "Mollusk." He jokingly called Plato the "Golden One." Democritus, among his peers, was called "The Mocker" because he was always making fun of human nature. The use of satire and cheerfulness in addressing each other produces intimacy and informality among friends. It serves as a social lubricant.

All of these elements help to confer pride in the tradition being passed down and in one's lineage, and ultimately preserves and strengthens it. In philosophy, this system would require a commonly-accepted standard curriculum of study after which graduations would take place. The usefulness of this system for the continuity of the Epicurean tradition is self-evident: it would produce knowledgeable, passionate philosophers.

I wish to accentuate the importance of wisdom traditions by citing a personal example that illustrates how useful it is to have access to the accumulated wisdom of others. After eight years of steady employment in the banking industry, I was one of the thousands of people who lost their jobs during the fall of 2008 as a result of Wall Street's excesses and crimes. As a result of this, I was in strong solidarity with the Occupy movement, which branded Wall Street "America's financial Gomorrah." I didn't just become radicalized politically: I was hurting. It was difficult for me to see the American dream crumble, to realize that many of my goals for the future were dissipating and that someday soon I may not even be able to afford my own home.

I've always loved to gather nuggets of wisdom from here and there. Today, I do not agree with many of the teachings of many of my former gurus and teachers, but when I did find wisdom, I gathered it. I journaled or blogged about it and made it my own. It was during the years of destitution that I found solace in this teaching:

The season of failure is the best time to sow the seeds of success.
—Paramahansa Yogananda

Yogananda had founded the Self Realization Fellowship in the middle of the twentieth century and I had gone through SRF's correspondence course to learn yoga. I had read and enjoyed many of the books by Yogananda, and although many of his teachings no longer resonated, some of the wisdom he imparted was exactly what I needed to hear at this juncture. What I like about the "season of failure" maxim is that it evokes imagery prevalent in Epicurean tradition, having to do with seeds, with Gardens, with how when we plant a seed or perform a deed, we will not immediately see the fruits. Things produced by our efforts come in their own time, and we have to be wise and patient.

It's during the season of failure that I decided to reinvent myself, to acquire new skills, a new outlook, and a new willingness to pursue unconventional careers and streams of income, including the skills that led to the writing of this book. The adage helped to bring me into what's being called the positive psychology movement, which focuses on the mind in its healthy state rather than in its diseased state. Epicureanism, in fact, is an ancient tradition of positive psychology where abiding pleasures are seen as our natural state.

If Yogananda had not founded his organization, and if his organization had not continued his teaching mission, this wisdom tradition would not have helped to give me a light at the end of the tunnel in one of my darkest hours to sustain me in my difficulties. Sowing the seeds of success is, indeed, the wisest thing to do during the season of failure. Lamenting won't help. Praying may help us to find and articulate our thoughts and emotions, but if it's not accompanied with pragmatic action it won't help either.

By sharing the example of Yogananda's maxim, I wish to stress that when you gather nuggets of wisdom and slowly develop our own wisdom tradition over the years, wisdom will settle in your head and no one can take away the wealth and the consolations of wit: it walks with you forever like a charm that protects you, like a guardian angel. Therefore, everyone should cultivate and value wisdom.

In order for an Epicurean revival to be successful, we should develop, nurture, and celebrate our individual and collective wisdom traditions, as well as develop ways in which to pass these down to the next generation.

The Teaching Mission

Epicurus taught that philosophy that does not heal the soul is no true philosophy and is no better than medicine that cannot cure the body. Giving people teachings about human happiness and avoidance of suffering is seen as a philanthropic mission; a mission which contends with the accusation, repeated often throughout history, that Epicureanism is a purely self-indulgent philosophy of selfish hedonism. A proper introduction to how Epicureans deal with desires will lay that stereotype to rest. Epicureanism is the only missionary secular humanist philosophy that Greece gave us, where converts were instructed to "each one teach one" and their households were centers of learning and teaching. There is a strong element of altruism in the Epicurean tradition: we aim to impart Epicurus' teachings as medicine for the soul.

The mission of the modern Society of Friends of Epicurus is to be true to the philanthropic spirit of the ancient Gardens: to spread a message that ultimately helps to liberate humanity from ignorance and unnecessary suffering.

The name of Epicurus translates as "ally" or "friend." We see him as a spiritual ally and a herald to humanists who are seeking to create beautiful, pleasant lives using the tool of philosophy. There are two premises at work here:

1. If we assume that Epicurus was a man of integrity whose deeds matched his words and stated beliefs (a premise which we have no reason to doubt), and
2. if we assume that he believed that pleasure guides the actions of righteous men, then
3. we can conclude that pleasure guided his choice to become, through his teachings, a sustaining, guiding presence for other mortals

We can understand that the teaching mission of the Gardens is, therefore, pleasurable and has the cultivation of abiding pleasure as one of its goals. This can be understood by considering how we derive pleasure from wholesome association with dear friends, as this was the context within which the teaching was originally imparted. The teaching mission must serve as the starting point to construct mutual aid societies where people help each other live pleasant lives.

It is impossible to ascertain what Epicurean communities might look like in the future, but some thinkers have expanded the notion of the social contract so that it is more than just about a mutual agreement to "not harm or be harmed," as our sources have it, and so that it concerns maximizing mutual pleasure.

Contemporary French hedonist philosopher Michel Onfrey articulates this notion of the social contract in terms of a utilitarian hedonism, one that pays attention to *our* pleasure rather than *my* pleasure, to the common good and to mutual interests rather than individual ones.

Utilitarian hedonism wants the calculation of joys with the goal of attaining the most benefits for one and the other.
—Michel Onfrey (my translation)

This is of extreme importance for many reasons. People who favor ascetic models of ethics want the world to believe that pleasure will always be accompanied with unpleasantness and inconvenience and that it's best to avoid pleasure. We reject that notion as a denial of life and of self, but then it falls to us to demonstrate how one's own affirmation *is* also the affirmation of the other.

Utilitarian hedonism is opposed, according to Onfrey, to vulgar or selfish (immature) hedonism not by being selfless or based on some other false virtue but by being mature and calculated. Perhaps he's on to something. Might our tradition contain the seed for a progressive form of communal covenant based on the doctrine of the social contract? How might the utilitarian hedonist theory be implemented in communities of philosopher-friends?

Epicurus embodies, to us, the ideals of philosophical friendship. As a prototype of the ideal friend, he dedicated his time on earth to helping people create a pleasant, tranquil life, and in return, he encouraged his followers to be a similarly kind, well-wishing presence for others in the same way that he was. Although he lived in a previous era, we can enjoy his association indirectly through his writings, legacy and teachings.

Wisdom as a Value

The Society of Friends of Epicurus seeks to give philosophy again a place of honor. Its devaluation, we believe, is a demoralizing and dehumanizing fact of history. Our narratives are and must be, in part, intended to help ensure the continuity of philosophy as a culturally vibrant and relevant aspect of human civilization and progress for all future generations.

This imperative of restoring our cultural and spiritual treasure requires conviction in the value of wisdom itself and, in my humble opinion, an accurate appreciation of the harm that was done to humanity when the Library of Alexandria was destroyed, when the philosophical schools were closed and for over a thousand years the people succumbed to the superstition, ignorance, misery and feudal slavery of the Dark Ages, from which we still have not made a full recovery. We must insist in the need for a humanist/naturalist historical perspective and narrative.

Some forms of wisdom are necessary and natural. Epicurus argued that without knowledge of science and of the true nature of things, we easily fall for the religious consensus that weather phenomena, thunder, earthquakes and astronomical movements are divinely ordained and, like death and the gods, should be feared. Science, insofar as it leads to emancipation from superstitious views and false beliefs that are detrimental to our soul and inspire fear, is considered natural and necessary knowledge for humans. This is plainly established in the Principal Doctrines.

Knowledge that is unattainable, burdensome, that is detrimental to a pleasant character, generates unnecessary pain or feeds our vanity should be considered vain and empty, and dismissed. This includes gossip, trash TV and other trashy or perturbing media.

If we are confused about the value of some form of knowledge, we should apply the same criteria as with anger or desires: is it natural and necessary for life, peace, health or safety? Otherwise, we run the risk of at least wasting a considerable and unrecoverable amount of time in needless pursuits. In this case, because we are dealing with knowledge, the risk of mental anxiety is the most significant potential repercussion of not analyzing our thirst for knowledge.

In conclusion: we must concern ourselves, primarily, with wisdom that has been established as natural and necessary, wisdom that leads to a pleasant and tranquil life, to health, and to happiness. We believe that our philosophical tradition classifies as natural and necessary knowledge; that it responds to the moral imperatives of life, health, happiness, safety, and even survival. Therefore, true wisdom is equal in value to pleasure and life, our ultimate end. The idea that man lives by his wits is also repeated in many other wisdom traditions.

The Twentiers: the People of Epicurus

Ancient Epicureans celebrated the twentieth (*eikas*) of every month, which is why they were known as the "Twentiers," and honored Epicurus' birthday in January. The tradition was originally established by Epicurus in his will in memory of both himself and Metrodorus.

The first teachers of Epicureanism advised that we should honor sages and virtuous persons because of the great benefits of wholesome association, and they acknowledged the need for wholesome moral mentors and role models. If and when Epicureans praise and pay honors to someone, the honored person invariably personifies imperturbability, equanimity, and a blissful existence.

It's been said that Epicurus declared the celebration of the twentieth of every month in order to coincide with the cult of Apollo and with the Eleusinian Mysteries, which also took place on the twentieth. Another possibility is that Epicurus wanted to make sure that his followers were not wasting time with these popular cults and that, instead, they fully dedicated themselves to philosophy. The cult at Eleusis, in particular, was very attractive and its mysteries promised everlasting life. Epicurus' rejection of an afterlife would have been inconsistent with Eleusinian mysteries. Therefore, holding meetings on the twentieth would have been the equivalent of philosophers today holding Sunday morning gatherings to make sure that their pupils are not also going to church or sending their children to Sunday school.

This consideration leads to another point worth noting: in the Jewish tradition, it is said that not only have the Jews kept the Sabbath but the Sabbath has kept the Jews. In other words, the reason for the survival of the collective memory and identity of Jewish people throughout such a long history and in spite of so much persecution has to do with the faithful keeping of the commandment of the Sabbath, which has protected their identity and memory as a people from being erased.

Eikas is the Epicurean Sabbath, and just as Sabbath kept the Jews who kept the Sabbath, so would *eikas* keep the Epicureans. We cannot truly call ourselves a living cultural tradition unless and until we keep the feasts of *euphraino* (broadly translated as the pleasures of the mind) on the twentieth of every month. We can speak of Epicurean history, and even of a vibrant literary and intellectual tradition, but we cannot truly speak of a cultural tradition unless there is contemporary culture and community built around the ideas of Epicureanism. *Eikas* IS our Tradition, and for as long as we celebrate the twentieth, we will continue to have a living tradition rather than entertain an intellectual curiosity.

Furthermore, the twentieth can be more than just a feast of reason and of simple foods. It can serve to reinvigorate our narratives and be turned into a day for learning and practicing simple, abiding pleasures: gratitude, study, singing, contemplation, and engaging friends in philosophical discourse.

Task: Celebrate the Twentieth

*The same conviction which inspires confidence that nothing
we have to fear is eternal or even of long duration, also
enables us to see that in the limited evils of this life nothing
enhances our security so much as friendship.*
—Principal Doctrine 28

Find ways to celebrate friendship. Use birthdays, the twentieth of each month, and any other excuse you find, to honor your friends by exchanging gifts and enjoying quality time.

XIV

FIRMLY GROUNDED IN REALITY: OUR
SCIENTIFIC COSMOLOGY

Co-Dependent Origination and Disintegration

Although this is a Buddhist doctrine, the idea of co-dependent arising is in line with Epicurean philosophy. In Buddhism, it culminates in a theory of no-self and, to us, it sheds light on the universality of impermanence and disintegration. Everything that emerges must eventually dissolve. In the third book of *De Rerum Natura*, Lucretius denies common pagan theories about the afterlife and offers a scientific, atomic alternative:

> Outcrowded by the new gives way, and ever
> The one thing from the others is repaired.
> Nor no man is consigned to the abyss
> Of Tartarus, the black. For stuff must be,
> That thus the after-generations grow,
> Though these, their life completed, follow thee;
> And thus like thee are generations all
> Already fallen, or some time to fall.
> So one thing from another rises ever;
> And in fee-simple life is given to none,
> But unto all mere usufruct.

In Epicurean doctrine, the path to insight about co-dependent origination was strictly atomic and death represents our tax to nature so that other living entities may have their chance to live. Like the word itself suggests, matter (*materia*) is the mother of all things and the birther of all phenomena: atoms are the seeds or building blocks of all things. If we break things down to progressively smaller particles, we will see that our bodies are made up of tissue, which is made up of cells, which are made up of molecules, which are made up of atoms. The earth is made up of rocks and water and other things, which are made up of molecules, which are made up of atoms, and so forth. All things can be broken down to the atomic level.

Epicurus also accurately taught that atoms are simple and that things only acquire their identifying properties (heat, color, taste, etc.) in the process of gaining complexity. Because all bodies are made up of progressively smaller things, their existence and their reality are dependent on their causes and components. Although composite things have properties and some are more stable than others, they lack an essence that is unchanging or eternal because their atoms can be recycled and become part of other bodies. This is particularly true of living beings who must constantly breathe, consume, and excrete in order to survive. We are all woven into a net of inter-being where all things emerge in this co-dependent manner, change, and eventually disintegrate.

We awaken to the fact that all the atoms in our bodies used to exist in beings that are long dead. We are made of recycled atoms from bodies of dinosaurs and other animals that no longer exist, microscopic organisms, plants, bodies of water, heavenly bodies, all the way down to the stardust we originally emerged from.

By contemplating on this doctrine and on the universality of impermanence and fully assimilating their insights, we are better able to accept things just as they are, including constant change in our world and, ultimately, our own inevitable mortality. Death is not the "wages of sin" as the Pauline school of Christianity teaches and it's not a deity or an angel as many aboriginals and Mexican Catholics think. Change and death are the completely natural results of birth. Everything that is born must die, as is in evidence in all of nature.

The Doctrine of Innumerable Worlds

Epicurus, and indeed it seems all the atomists, believed in

the doctrine of innumerable worlds. The first source where it is expounded is Epicurus' Epistle to Herodotus:

> Moreover, there is an infinite number of worlds, some like this world, others unlike it. For the atoms being infinite in number, as has just been proved, are borne ever further in their course. For the atoms out of which a world might arise, or by which a world might be formed, have not all been expended on one world or a finite number of worlds, whether like or unlike this one. Hence there will be nothing to hinder an infinity of worlds.

Later, in the second chapter of his poem *On the Nature of Things*, Lucretius boldly concludes the following after pondering the infinitude of atoms and of possible combinations of atoms and bodies:

> There are other worlds in other parts of the universe and other races of men and of wild beasts.

A prominent Epicurean of the second century by the name Diogenes of Oeananda, who built a large wall in his home city and adorned it with Epicurean inscriptions, later mentions the doctrine in his *Letter to Antipater*.

> I am sending you, in accordance with your request, the arguments concerning an infinite number of worlds. This doctrine came to be better articulated as a result of being turned over between the two of us face to face; for our agreements and disagreements with one another, and also our questionings, rendered the inquiry into the object of our search more precise. The dialogue began something like this: "Diogenes," said Theodoridas, "that the doc-

trine laid down by Epicurus on an infinite number
of worlds is true I am confident"

Materialist philosophers appear to have derived this idea
from the belief in the infinity of the cosmos. The sheer mathematics of such a cosmos would inherently carry within it
countless possibilities.

Now that we've cited the sources for this fascinating
teaching, let's continue the process that Diogenes and The-
odoridas were engaged in of assessing, clarifying, and updating this doctrine in light of contemporary research. As the
centuries have advanced, scientists and mathematicians have
made progressively more accurate attempts at identifying
how many worlds are out there, although we have been able
to confirm only thousands of exoplanets (worlds outside our
solar system).

According to calculations carried out at the University of
New South Wales (Anthony, 2003), at least 25 percent of sun-
like stars have planets, which would mean there are at least
100 billion stars with planets in our galaxy, and with about
100 billion galaxies in the observable universe, there would
be at least 10 trillion planetary systems in the known universe. Many of these stars, like our own, have multiple planets
and moons.

In addition to mathematical models employed to determine how many planets might exist, there is one model used
to determine how many civilizations able to communicate
exist in the cosmos: the Drake Equation, which was devised
by Dr. Frank Drake. However, depending on what numbers
we choose to enter as its variables, we may get wildly diverging
amounts of intelligent civilizations.

Corroborations on the existence and number of exoplanets (that is, planets outside our solar system) have been coming
in since the 1990s. Some of these worlds have been discovered
by astronomers and researchers working independently in all
parts of the world, while others have been discovered as part

of exoplanetary research being carried out by Kepler and other telescopes specifically created for such a task. In only a few years, Kepler has already found over 1,200 exoplanets–over 50 of them orbiting within the habitable zone, the region that is not too hot or too cold to harbor life—and that was only by observing the nearest stars within a small fraction of the sky.

But if it's life we're looking for, then we would need to account for the numbers of habitable moons also. Some of the planets in our own solar system have dozens of moons. What if there is a moon like Pandora out there, or like the Star Wars' forest moon of Endor? Adding moons to the equation would again multiply the final results. By even the most conservative estimates, the cosmos has trillions of planets and moons, and is teeming with potentially habitable worlds.

In addition to saving mortals from irrational fears about our ultimate fate, the study of astronomy and cosmology governed by natural laws adds awe, beauty, splendor, humility, conviction, respect for science, and many more spiritual values to our Epicurean faith.

If we gaze at a small portion of the sky for even five minutes, in any direction we look, we should know that we are looking at millions of worlds; that there are countless planetary systems in our own galaxy, and beyond them there are countless far away galaxies; that they are innumerable like grains of sand.

Although we may choose to think of our cities as mold, as a giant bacteria that is taking over our world, we may also choose the alternate view that we are intelligent tiny mammalian germs holding on to the skin of our blue planet and, as it whirls in space, we're able to have the intelligence to understand more or less accurately our place within it, and in the future we may have the power to expand beyond the blue planet.

What a unique and marvelous opportunity, to be members of a species that has awakened to intelligence and to an accurate, scientific cosmology after four billion years of life on earth! Although the remoteness of these worlds may seem to make them irrelevant, we are fortunate to have a chance to spend a short amount of time in this universe awakening to it as humans.

At Home in Our Cosmos

The contemplative practice of stargazing and learning about our cosmos is a source of awe, but it also provides us with the added value of a coherent, ever-expanding cosmology. A science-based cosmology accepts updates to it as we discover new things and becomes a never-ending didactic adventure, whereas a religious or mythical cosmology is threatened by ever-expanding knowledge. There is, literally, an infinite amount to learn about our universe. There is no end to how fascinating the adventure of reality can be.

We also should not fool ourselves into thinking that astronomy provides the boundaries in the quest for knowledge. All around us and below us are universes to explore. We know little about the depths of our oceans, where no light can reach, but from what has been observed it is an entirely other dimension where pressures would kill most land-bound animals, yet these depths are populated by strange creatures that exhibit bioluminescence.

The animal and plant worlds above the waters are also an endless source of fascination. Ants, as tiny and easy to ignore as they are, live complex social lives in societies marked by class distinctions and ruled by a single monarch. They engage in war and in slavery, they harvest fungi and other sources of foods, they communicate using chemicals and are brilliant architects able to build structures with complex ventilation systems. And we are now beginning to understand the chemical signals used by plants to communicate with each other as well as their sleep cycles and other attributes that, before, were only associated with animal behavior.

The acceptance of the secure foundation of a science-based cosmology and philosophy requires no suspension of our convictions, as the expansion in our knowledge of the cosmos will never threaten our worldview. It is therefore to be expected that Epicureanism as an ethical guide based on the study of nature will continue to evolve and remain relevant just as it has during the last 2,300 years.

During the days of Constantine, an attempt at creating a globalized worldview resulted in the creation of the Roman Catholic Church, which led to the eventual silencing of all its dissidents, and ultimately degenerated into the dawn of the Dark Ages. The word "catholic" may mean universal, but no amount of imperial domination can produce a cosmology that will pass the test of observable facts and be worthy of the label universal.

The paranoid leaders of the church may have persecuted scientists and intimidated people into full submission during the Middle Ages, but no amount of bullying can change the fact that their untruths in the end were proven to be the false doctrines that they are. The earth is still round, it's still not the center of the universe, and snakes still do not talk. We may be gullible enough to believe the Catholic doctrines of Christ's and the virgin's physical ascent to heaven ... but gravity will still pull us.

History and science have taught us that, even if through conquest people of different beliefs and tribes can come together under one faith and experience solidarity, truth is not a matter of who dominates the world just as it is not a matter to be voted on.

Epicurus' advice to live unknown exhibits the confidence of a teacher who knows he will be vindicated at some point in history. He accurately saw that we would not need political power to gain relevance. A scientific cosmology does not require the bullying of others. Who needs intimidation when there is evidence?

Since Constantine, there have been more recent attempts by false Platonic doctrines and religions to create a coherent, harmonious cosmology and worldview for a globalized era, one that resolves the cognitive dissonance that arises from trying to find semantics for all the peoples of the world to effectively communicate in spite of their different worldviews. Prominent among them is the Baha'i Faith, an amalgam of beliefs from Islam, Christianity, Hinduism and other faiths. It claims that all the religions are inspired by the One God ... but fails to clarify how Hindu reincarnation and the notions of heaven and hell in Abrahamic religions can fit within one worldview, or how the Buddhist doctrine of *anatta* (non-being) and the near-universal belief in the existence of an immortal soul in other faiths can fit within a single worldview.

Even prior to Constantine, ancient Ptolemaic pharaohs had promoted the cult of Serapis, a deity who was an amalgam of Greek and Egyptian symbols, in order to unify Greeks and barbarians in his kingdom. Serapis was to be the great unifier of all humanity. But where is the cult of Serapis today? It's obsolete. Unlike Erastothenes' measurement of the circumference of the earth, which also took place in Egypt, the cult was made obsolete by the passing of its culture and by the illegitimacy of its supernatural claims. The earth, however, is still round. Erastothenes, a mere mortal, proved to be much greater and immortal than the god Serapis.

A better, safer, time-tested alternative is to put aside the Platonic views that have resulted only in failure to accurately describe reality for millennia and to embrace a cosmology that is rooted in reality and that is informed by science, one that will not lose relevance and that will prove intellectually and spiritually satisfying thousands of years into the future. We do not live in the cosmos that was imagined by ancient Sumerians or ancient Egyptians ... but people of all the ages have lived and will always live in the progressively richer cosmos that is being explained in increasing detail by science.

Epicurus calls us and initiates us into the maturity of our species. He gave us the clarity of a rational, scientific, coherent worldview in a cosmopolitan world torn by disparate, incompatible cosmo-visions that do not fit together and sometimes clash; a worldview that evolves along with science and observable facts about reality. We can find ourselves here in our cosmos, with our feet firmly planted on the ground, and create meaning and value without the cognitive dissonance that globalization induces.

For this reason, whether we are curious to learn more and enjoy star-gazing or whether we value the serenity and simplicity of this doctrine and wish to remain settled in ataraxia, even after all these centuries we can all still enjoy the stable foundation that Epicurus' scientific cosmology provides.

The End of Days

Shortly after his argument in favor of other worlds with other races towards the end of his second book, Lucretius goes on to discuss the countless amount of stars and heavenly bodies, and concludes that just as all biological bodies come to an end, so with all heavenly bodies.

Then is the time when everything comes to a stop
and nature reins back any further increase.
For when anything that you see is growing happily
and gradually, step by step, approaches maturity,
it is taking in more elements than it gives out,
for food is readily taken into its veins
and it is not so laxly made that it loses particles
faster than the ages can replace them.

By observing nature, Lucretius came to an insight into impermanence as it can be applied to all heavenly bodies and philosophically approached a version of what our folk myths have called *Ragnarok*, or the Apocalypse.

End-of-days prophecies, like death and the gods, have been a source of perturbed religious imagery and fear for thousands of years. Epicurus encouraged the study of science as a remedy against irrational fears based on false opinions inspired by religion and superstition. The ethical purpose of the study of these matters is to ensure that we remain fearless and unperturbed.

We know that our sun is kept alive by fusion, but one day it will burn up all its fuel and die. Thankfully our day of doom, when the sun will expand, swallow the earth, and explode into a supernova is billions of years away and, unless another cataclysm visits us first, there is an abundance of time to prepare heavenly Gardens in other planets for our distant descendants. Ultimately, if future generations are to pragmatically face this challenge, they must become celestial Gardeners and take life (and, I must add, philosophy) to other planets, terraform and colonize them. Otherwise humans will inevitably become extinct like the dinosaurs.

The universality of impermanence, and our scientific understanding of stars, make this day of doom a necessary feature of our cosmology. Everything that is born, must die. But just as other traditions speak of a new heaven and a new earth, or of new ages of humanity in the case of Mayans and Hindus, the humanist tradition can and should articulate its own highest hopes for the far future after the end of days where science would come to the rescue. In fact, science fiction folklore has already begun our species' ethical conversation and scientific speculation about our far future.

Task: Make a Pilgrimage to a Planetarium

For the sake of wonder, you may visit museums of natural history and learn about the nature of things. But planetariums awaken a peculiar fascination. They literally expand our cosmos and our horizons.

References

Anthony, Sebastian. "Astronomers estimate 100 billion habitable earth-like planets in the Milky Way, 50 sextillion in the universe." *ExtremeTech*, April 4, 2013. Retrieved from http:// www.extremetech.com/extreme/152573-astronomers-esti- mate-100-billion-habitable-earth-like-planets-in-the-milky- way-50-sextillion-in-the-universe

Lucretius Carus, Titus. *De Rerum Natura*. Leonard, William E. (Trans.). Retrieved from http://classics.mit.edu/Carus/ nature_things.html

XV

HEAVEN ON EARTH

The tradition of philosophical materialism teaches that whatever spiritual or transcendental reality exists, is anchored in matter ... and that it is pointless to entertain hopes for an idyllic afterlife (or fear a hellish one) rather than discover, build and co-create paradise here and now on Earth.

It is this imperative that inspires our teaching mission. We hold the belief that philosophy and its fruits are worth sharing, that it is desirable to live in a society teeming with wise, tranquil, happy, wholesome philosophers, that it is desirable—and a moral imperative—to live among wise autarchs who embody and exemplify the ideals of friendship and self-sufficiency and to create around us a heavenly, godly subculture. We may not hold the utopian, naive belief that such a planetary civilization is possible without coercion and that everyone will exhibit the virtues of philosophy, but we believe it's possible for pockets of humanity to live in Garden-like bliss.

By assuming the teaching mission, we expand the possibility of innumerable sentient beings experiencing a pleasant life here on earth, and while we make the resolution to be happy with or without externals, we also choose freely to contribute to the creation of Gardens and to turning much of the Earth itself into a Garden conducive to a pleasant life. This is, potentially, the great gift of the ethical materialist tradition of philosophy as embodied in Epicureanism. Our heaven, our paradise narrative is not in the after-life. It is in life, in nature.

The sister school of materialism from India, known as the *Carvakas*, teaches that both heaven and hell exist here on planet Earth and nowhere else. They're not in the heavenly planets, but they're not imaginary either. They believe that there are hellish places in our world such as slaughterhouses, workplaces and relationships founded on abuse and exploitation, as well as societies plagued by violence, ignorance, oppression and warfare—but there are also heavenly places of joy and beauty where people relate to each other lovingly and with kindness, where there's safety and wisdom.

An extension of this belief is that there are angels and demonic personalities in the flesh. They don't dwell in the imaginal realm, but here on earth. There are people who have such strong prevalence of negative habits that they're, for all purposes, demons: the parasitical and exploitative bosses, the rapists, the thieves, and violent criminals. On the other hand, we all have guardian angels, people whose love always protects us. There are angel dogs that guide the blind, angel firefighters and doctors who save lives, angel teachers who, like Epicurus, mentor us and wish us well, leading us to a happy and pleasant existence.

Towards the end of the third book of *On the Nature of Things*, Lucretius also makes comparisons between the mythical creatures and scenes of the afterlife used to instill fear in mortals and the worldly counterparts of those terrible things. He argues, for instance, that while there is no Tantalus scared that a rock may fall on him, men who fear gods are haunted by comparable fears; that while there is no Tityos pecked at by birds in Acheron, a similar anguish is felt by a neglected lover or a man victimized by his desires; that Sisyphus' eternal push of a heavy stone uphill can be compared to men blindly seeking after power. Mythical legends, when appropriated by philosophy, prove useful metaphors for life in this world and have been used didactically in our tradition.

Epicurus advised people to contemplate the gods as embodiments of ataraxia and of the virtues of philosophy. Diogenes of Oeananda argued that statues of the gods should smile. What are we to make of Catholic statues on whose faces martyrdom and misery are positively glorified and dignified? Having grown up Catholic, I was used to denial of life and pleasure, as represented in the agony in the faces of its saints, and it never occurred to me that spiritual imagery should be uplifting and happy until I saw a beautiful, serene, blissful smiling Buddha figure one day in a Zen temple.

Mahayana Buddhism has sacred writings and sutras that describe in detail the innumerable blissful Buddha-lands that have been created by the virtue and effort of countless awakened beings. By contemplating an Epicurean heaven filled with blissful gods through art, literature, and imagery, we admire and can learn to emulate godly behavior. The poet Lucretius, who likened Epicurus to a divinity, defined godliness as including any exemplary behavior that led to the practice of the heroic virtues of philosophy.

A clear, tangible model for what the pleasant life feels like would help to formulate a pleasant life in practice. We should therefore attempt to imagine paradise in all its details. This, I anticipate, will help us to understand Epicurean teachings on how the good is easy to attain and how we already live in a place that can lead to a blissful existence.

Task: Envision Heaven

It is impossible to create a better society without first attempting to accurately and clearly flesh out its defining details, and then figuring out what it takes to either find or manifest those details in our surroundings. The following exercise should help to establish in our collective imagination and in our artistic expression the aspirations that we wish to entertain and to attain as we begin to, again, establish Epicurean Gardens in modern society.

Use your imagination and your journal, not just once but several times, to articulate what heaven-on-earth feels like here and now. Do not think in hypothetical terms (what if ...) but, instead, be in a creative space where you feel, smell, enjoy, relish and live in this paradise as if it was already in front of you, as if it was your immediate surroundings. You may draw inspiration from your favorite movies or from paintings, art, etc. If money, education and societal conventions were no obstacle, how would we co-create paradise on earth?

How does paradise feel? What does it look like ... what architecture, what natural features does it have? Are the streets clean? Is the air fresh? What aromas exist there? You may find pictures in publications that resonate with your imagery of paradise. If you collect them, that may help to make paradise more tangible to you. It may serve to remind you of the highest destiny that you'd like to create.

As you place yourself in the midst of heaven, what are the specific characters that inhabit your heavenly existence? Do people treat each other affectionately? How often do people laugh? Surely they do not take themselves seriously at all times!

What kinds of activities do people engage in? How do they enjoy leisure? Surely they don't work all the time! What beautiful background music do you hear? Would there be dance, arts, etc.? How often? Are these things valued? How do people use science?

What types of delicious food are eaten in paradise? How is this food produced? Do people exercise frequently? How? In what ways are people healthy and physically vibrant?

Fully indulge your imagination. Focus on the things that matter most to you, but don't forget the simple, day to day pleasures.

Ponder that Earth is a tiny blue world whirling in space and that we orbit, already, in heaven after all. We are in heaven. Why not live up to it?

And finally, ponder how these visions of heaven might influence both your short- and long-term chosen projects for your life, whether you get involved in social or environmental justice movements or whether you are literally a gardener or architect. How do you think you can help manifest the beauty you envision? How can you help others who are near and dear to you gain the wealth or happiness that you envision? What other projects or activities can you embrace that will help you live closer to your ideal?

The end result of this exercise should be a tendency to affect and co-create our world accordingly. We know that we do not have to do things the way they've been done traditionally. How, then, do we do them?

The moral superiority of a philosophical school should be measured, in part, by its ability to help individuals and communities effectively create some form of heaven on earth.

Task: Find Paradise in Your World

During the writing of this book, I sought refuge in places in nature in order to focus and to be inspired by a pleasant environment. I discovered the simple pleasure of lying on the grass in the north side of Chicago on a small hill between the bike paths, between the highway and Lake Michigan surrounded by trees. Amid a green bed with golden flowers, I saw the trees begin to green in early summer and in the late summer, I saw the dragonflies mating. And I heard the song of the water just below and to the side.

I spent hours there and realized that most people take this beautiful, peaceful place for granted. People run, skate, and bike all around the site, but few venture into the grass, which serves as a natural cushion. I'm able to be productive and do a lot of reading, writing and brainstorming there.

It's there that I thought about the notion of earthly paradise and how we fail to identify it even when it's right under our noses. I've felt a sense of being in paradise in many places: visiting sites with gardens and architectural grandeur, having a lazy Sunday afternoon at the beach, and even enjoying the high-energy nights in downtown Chicago when the city lights make the buildings look like Gotham City.

Journal about the paradise in your world. Where and when have you felt a sense of being surrounded by a heavenly realm?

If you're an extrovert, I encourage you to think in visual terms but if you're a visual thinker, I encourage you to also think in relational terms: Who creates paradise for you? What friends or family members make you feel happy regardless of where you are? Who makes you laugh easily? There are people that we love so much that they immediately make us feel safe. They are also part of our Paradise.

Conclusion

Let no one delay the study of philosophy while he is young, and when he is old let him not become weary of the study; for no man can ever find the time unsuitable or too late to study the health of his soul.

—Epicurus

Tending the Garden is a lifelong process for an individual, and for the human race it was a project that lasted seven centuries, went through a hiatus of 1,500 years, and is now again beginning. Therefore, most of the pages of this book have not yet been written.

Think of this book as an initiation into the process of tending the garden of the soul. My hope is that what started as a discussion about the imperative of cultivating prudence will continue in your daily lives and help you flourish, igniting an inner revolution.

While many of the economically disenfranchised in our society call for solidarity with labor, with Occupy Wall Street and other such movements, and while there is merit to these calls for solidarity, Epicurus calls us to the truly revolutionary task of Occupying Our Souls. He calls us to be in control of our desires, to apply cognitive therapy in the slaying of the monsters of the soul, and to mindfully and diligently plan to live pleasant lives in the company of wholesome friends. The real revolution starts within. This is not a task that many are ready for, but my challenge is to see the process as an adventure.

It was my intention in writing the book to set the foundation for the future work of the Society of Friends of Epicurus and to encourage you, my readers, to engage in philosophical discourse within yourselves and with your friends, to develop your own wisdom traditions and, regardless of whether or not you assume an Epicurean outlook in life, to draw inspiration from our school's master, Epicurus. One does not have to be doctrinally an Epicurean to learn about and celebrate his legacy. I hope you have been well entertained with this book and found as much pleasure in reading it as I did in writing it!

Please learn more about our tradition at:

societyofepicurus.com
newepicurean.com
epicurus.info

CPSIA information can be obtained at www.ICGtesting.com
Printed in the USA
BVOW06s1921170216

437112BV00011B/115/P

9 780931 779534